The Bridge

Geert Mak

The Bridge

A Journey Between Orient
and Occident

TRANSLATED FROM THE DUTCH BY

Sam Garrett

Harvill Secker
LONDON

Published by Harvill Secker 2008

First published in The Netherlands in 2007 by
Stichting Collectieve Propaganda van het Nederlandse Boek

English translation © Sam Garrett 2008

2 4 6 8 10 9 7 5 3 1

Copyright © Geert Mak 2007

Geert Mak has asserted his right under the Copyright,
Designs and Patents Act 1988 to be identified as the author of this work

First published in Great Britain in 2008 by
HARVILL SECKER
Random House, 20 Vauxhall Bridge Road
London SW1V 2SA

www.rbooks.co.uk

Addresses for companies within The Random House Group Limited
can be found at: www.randomhouse.co.uk/offices.htm

The Random House Group Limited Reg. No. 954009

A CIP catalogue record for this book is available from the British Library

ISBN 9781846551383

The publishers are grateful for the support of the Foundation
for the Production and Translation of Dutch Literature

Foundation for the
Production and
Translation of
Dutch Literature

The Random House Group Limited supports The Forest Stewardship
Council (FSC), the leading international forest certification organisation.
All our titles that are printed on Greenpeace approved FSC certified paper carry
the FSC logo. Our paper procurement policy can be found at
www.rbooks.co.uk/environment

Printed and bound in Great Britain by
GGP Media GmbH, Pößneck, Germany

On the bridge you don't make friends,
from the bridge you watch and see.

Said Faik

I

On the bridge, everything is done in millions. 'Yesterday I caught twenty million worth, nothing but sardines.' 'Three million for the best picture you've ever had taken!' 'Two cups of tea, that's half a million, thank you.' 'I've been here since the crack of dawn, only four million, when's the money going to start crossing the bridge again?' 'Real Chanel, five million!'

The high voice of the lottery-ticket girl echoes down the arcade: 'Who's going for a hundred billion? Who will it be?' The shop window behind her is full of Zeus Super, Kral 2005 Magnum and Blue Compact pistols, to say nothing of the ladies' handguns, the elegant Geax en Class-minis; ten easy instalments of twenty-five million apiece put the power over life and death straight into your handbag.

The bridge offers everything anyone could want: combs, orthopaedic sandals, cigarettes, dancing dolls, Gucci bags and Rolexes for no more than, say, twenty million, Nokias of dubious provenance, umbrellas decorated with flowering fields, shaving brushes, condoms and crawling mechanical infantry-men who squeeze off a round every ten seconds.

A million comes to about fifty euro cents, it's out-dated coinage really, one of those hysterically inflating currencies from the last century. But the bridge has an exchange rate all of its own. And the fish are thrown in for free, a gift for being here. There are always dozens of rods jutting over the railing. Today is the day for fat sardines. For some strange reason huge schools of them are moiling about beneath the bridge – but next week all you'll reel in will be the odd fingerling. A determined-looking woman pulls up one sardine after another as the private boats and rusty tugs go growling beneath the bridge, and the pavement shakes and shimmies with the passing of the trams. She used to be a nurse, then she retired, now she does something with computers. She's been fishing here every day for the last ten years; within a couple of hours she will have caught dinner for the whole family. 'This is my way of meditating.' She lights a cigarette, hands me the huge casting rod. 'Try it, it's relaxing.' In the distance the tankers go shuffling by, the red bulk carriers heading from the Crimea to Europe, the white American cruise liners.

In the same way that other parts of the world have a dozen or more words for rain, snow or fog, this city knows at least thirty varieties of wind, and the fishermen have named them all. When the Pleasant Storm, the Storm of the Blackbirds or the Storm of the Cuckoos comes blowing in from the west, the spring will be mild and dry. Easterly winds with their morning mist, like the Storm of Fish, provide relief from the heat of summer and bring rain all year round. The Black Wind – which comes from the east as well, but only in winter – powders the city with snow. Now everyone is braced for the spring storms, the Storm of the Swallow and the Storm of Swans. The tourist season has started. They've planted three million tulips, everywhere you look there are tulips, even atop the bridge's control booths they stand swaying in the cold wind, fat plastic bubbles of red and yellow.

For the moment, however, all the weather still comes from the Black Sea, it's the Boreas that is blowing and showers fall incessantly. The fishermen have decked themselves out in sheets of plastic, worn tarpaulins and old fertiliser bags. The ferries putter back and forth in the greyness, gulls dive past, shiny black umbrellas go trundling across the bridge, its far end hidden behind a foggy white wall. The sonorous motors of the *Professor Aykut Barka* and the *Mehmet Ahif Ersoy* are idling along the northern quay, greasy black smoke shoots from their stacks, an abrupt turn of the rudder and the two ferries are off. On the TV screens in the cafés beneath the bridge tropical fish swim back and forth the livelong day. This is the only company one has today.

3

The entire populace of the bridge has retreated to the tunnels at either end. The side closest to the old city smells, as always, of fried fish, but there isn't a customer in sight. Rowdy with boredom this morning, the young cigarette vendors are kicking up their heels. Their insults are aimed at the foreigners or any other fool who happens to pass by. The perfume vendor has taken refuge in the lee of an old retaining wall. He's one of those fellows you sometimes see in a suit jacket many sizes too large for him, its pockets filled with fakeries, one of the characters you try to avoid while crossing the bridge, but with whom you fall into conversation anyway because it's raining and there's nothing else to do.

He talks about his village, he probably never talks about anything else. 'It was built up against the mountainside; twelve houses, some goats, sheep, a few potato patches, a beanfield for the army, sometimes tomatoes for the market in town, we squeaked by.' At the age of seven it was time for him to go to work, herding sheep in summer, gathering firewood until the first snow fell. 'We didn't have toys. We played with stones.'

His village no longer exists, all the families have moved away, it's even been deleted from the official records. The families grew too large to support – there were sometimes as many as ten or fifteen people living in one house – the village couldn't feed so many mouths. 'One winter night – I'll

4

never forget this – the village was besieged by a pack of wolves; they tore apart about twenty sheep. After that everyone left. What else could we do?'

The perfume vendor doesn't know what became of those twelve families. Most went to Europe, of course, one of them even went to Holland. He himself had gone to the city and found odd jobs: in a shooting gallery, a restaurant, a barber shop. He sold bottled water, fruit, fish, socks and wristwatches. He was married, divorced, now he has a room in a boarding house and lives for the rare Sunday afternoons when he and his young son walk the city together. The bridge is his destiny, there's nothing anyone can do about that. 'My family couldn't send me to school, they were too poor, it was that simple. I can pay my bills, I make ends meet, but I'm on my own, that's all.'

Lately, more than ever before, he has been spending his nights in that village of twelve houses; he hears the morning sounds – the twitter of birds, the bleating of sheep, the wind, the river – the grass rustles beneath his feet, he plays with his stones. Like a drowned cat, he waits for the rain to stop – tomorrow, the weather report says, for then there will be snow.

The bridge is not hard to identify. You come flying in over the city, over these ten million souls, their villas and tower blocks rolling away across the hillsides, over the inland seas and bays that divide the city, over the suspension bridges where the freight convoys between Europe and Asia grind along bumper to bumper, over the dozens of ships rusting eternally in the harbours, over the fallen bastions and city walls of the long-vanished empire, over the Blue Mosque, above which, in sharp relief against the evening sky, white birds are always flying. And then, unavoidably, your eye is drawn to the bridge.

Or else you discover it by accident. You walk down the narrow streets past the bazaar, past the cheeses, the olives, the display cases filled with jars of honey and fruit conserves, past the ironmongers' shops, the saws, the stoves and teapots, past the men standing solemnly beside their boxes full of ball-point pens and paper hankies, past the butchers with their sausage, tripe and goat heads, past the vendors of lottery tickets and luck. Or you follow the quay where the ferry boats dock; you fade into the vast morning masses rolling into the city, the young businessmen, the porters, the office girls, the farm-women, that whole parade of briefcases and threadbare suit jackets; you plough your way through the engines' throb, the fast tick of the girls' heels, the street merchants' shouts; the light reflects across the water, each day in a different way, always in motion; the gulls cry and, suddenly, there, round the corner, behind the kiosks and the stairways, begins the bridge.

The bridge, in fact, is not a pretty sight. Built of concrete, it is a little more than half a kilometre long, four lanes and a set of tram tracks wide, a counterweight construction at its middle, its access ramps surrounded by tunnels and shopping arcades. The paved surface climbs gradually, so that smaller boats can easily pass beneath in mid-river. Under the bridge, on the waterfront, lies a long row of restaurants and teahouses – pedestrians can also cross beneath the bridge itself; that's cosier, but halfway across, close to the control towers, you have to negotiate an extra set of steps. And of course you miss all that space, the sea, the autumn mists, the dolphins that on occasion roll up across a distant wave.

The bridge spans a broad estuary that divides the two oldest districts – and, with them, the two spirits living within this city: the southern shore is conservative and looks towards the East, while the northern side with its centuries-old embassies and merchants' palaces is permeated with the mentality of the West and the lightness of modern life.

A beloved chronicler of this city – we shall meet a few of them along our way – once compared the masses of houses in the two districts to the 'broad wingspan of a slender bird'. That image still applies. The bridge is the slim body between those massive wings. 'The bridge is slender, tiny, but take it away and those enormous wings will break off as well,

7

they will no longer be able to move, to soar into the air!'

Without the bridge you cannot know the city. The bridge is, in fact, a city, though one must not take that too literally; the bridge is not the city and the city is not the country, not by a long shot. The bridge is, above all, itself, and we shall leave it at that.

Now the bridge unfolds. The morning has rippled past, the rain has stopped. A shoeshiner has joined the crowd and a man acting as a kind of living free-ads paper. He is bound and determined to sell an almost-new electric drill; he stands on the walkway, the drill at his feet, the little set of drill bits beside it, and he waits. Everyone in this city waits, all the time, and sometimes it helps.

Down in the tunnel a new toy is being sold as well: miniature Smart cars that drive around to a cheerful tune and flap their doors like birds. Five million. In one corner three shiny new suitcases stand waiting for big adventures. An old beggar has taken a seat on the steps. If you stop to talk to him he will raise his head and point to a little steel plate at the base of his throat. That was where his voice resided, now it has been cut away for good.

The men who run the shell game are taking up their positions. This act of theirs involves a chair, a deck of cards and an old newspaper, and the rest is the same thing you see everywhere: a man who deals cards, around him two or three accomplices who clap their hands and do little dances to show that they've won and how happy they are about that, around them in turn a few pickpockets who skilfully fleece any stranger who happens to mingle with the group – insofar as the stranger hasn't already been robbed of all his money by the game itself. The men on the bridge, however, have over-looked one thing that gives them away: they all clearly come from the same part of the country, probably from the same family, they have the same leathery faces, the same dismal raincoats hanging halfway to their spindly knees; no dance can disguise that.

In 1878 the Italian writer Edmondo de Amicis walked across the bridge – the predecessor of the predecessor of today's bridge – with his gaze fixed on what was then the wooden surface and 'all the footwear of the world' that crossed it,

from the nakedness of Adam to the latest Parisian boots: the Turk's yellow slippers, the Armenian's red ones, the Greek's blue ones, the black slippers of the Israelite; sandals, boots from Turkestan, Albanian gaiters, low-cut shoes, the piebald *gambas* of the horsemen of Asia Minor, slippers embroidered with gold, Spanish *alpargatas*, footwear of satin, of rope,

9

of rags, of wood, all crowded together so closely that while you focus on one pair, hundreds of others escape your attention.

Almost one hundred and fifty years later I see an endless flow of sports shoes passing by, those of merchants, tourists, gamblers, pickpockets. I see waiters' black lace-ups. The dingy loafers of a porter lugging a huge basket of vegetables. The pavement photographer's white Pumas. The gold winkle-pickers and silver sandals of two self-conscious girls parading about in fashionable turquoise and orange dresses, their headscarves bright and colourful. The tanned bare feet – with black oil stains – of a glue sniffer. The no-nonsense clogs of a fundamentalist couple in black. The high-topped trainers in which a schoolgirl – bobbed hair, 'Life' T-shirt, satchel slung over one shoulder – gambols along. The silver slippers of a minuscule Mardi Gras prince, a little boy who is today celebrating his circumcision. The perfume vendor's worn leather brogues.

Edmondo de Amicis had to take care not to be knocked over, that's how busy it was on the bridge in his day. 'First a water bearer carrying a huge leather bag on his back, then a Russian lady on horseback or a company of quick-stepping imperial soldiers in the uniform of the *Zouave*, followed by a troop of Armenian porters, walking two by two, on their shoulders long staves from which hang enormous bales of merchandise.'

Today the activity on the bridge has been channelled: there is the tramway for the middle class, the road for the wealthy and the would-be rich, and the pavement for the losers, the tourists and dissidents. The pace of pedestrian traffic has slowed to something more like traipsing or strolling. And the fishermen never budge, an unthinkable phenomenon on de Amicis's lively bridge. In his day almost no one fished from the bridge, there were plenty of other places in the city where one could scoop the fish straight from the water. It was only in the 1980s, when the city was again confronted with mass unemployment, that the bridge became a popular fishing spot.

'You used to be able to go to the teahouse, play cards with your friends for a little money,' says a fisherman, one of the old guard, 'but in the end no one could afford that. So we started fishing. It costs almost nothing, you get something back for it as well, and look at how healthy I am, and how relaxed!' He's stopped working and these days you'll always find him on the bridge in his baseball cap and checked shirt. But he has never fished for profit; the same goes for most of the bridge's other anglers.

After getting to know them better, you discover that most are retired or hold an office job from which the bridge offers, above all, a few hours' holiday. 'Fishing every day is a lesson in patience,' says a man who works at a bank. 'It's become part of my world-view. And never giving up, not even at eight o'clock on a November evening with the rain washing away your bones, yes, damn it, that's part of it as well.' 'It's pure meditation,' says a woman who has problems at home. 'I always used to get stomach-aches from the stress, but the sea helped me through it.'

The elderly couple, who always fish beside the westernmost control tower, are one of the few exceptions. They only started about three years ago, but it's how they make their living. 'Of course it's possible,' he says, pulling up a bucket of water. 'In a good season, in fact, it's no trouble at all. But there are months when we catch almost nothing, then we're really in a tight spot.' They start at six o'clock each morning, earn ten or fifteen million a day, an average of about three hundred and fifty million a month. He carefully unravels a new length of line, she rolls him a cigarette, their little dog stays in his old carrier bag beside the bait bucket. The sea air has left them tanned. 'We have financial problems sometimes. One of our sons helps us out, of his own accord, he's doing quite well. The other children too, all three of them received an education. But we're not going to ask them for money!'

Then they start telling me about the day they met, so many years ago – it was in Venice, she was a Spanish factory girl, he was a footloose lorry driver – and how it went after that, first Spain, then the bridge. When they're together, they still beam.

All professional fishermen begin by catching bait. First the little fish are split down the middle, then the real work starts. 'But the big fish you had back when our parents were alive, you don't catch anything like that any more,' everyone will tell you. 'They're all pulled in by the trawlers, off the coast – and the water isn't any cleaner, either.' The man who works at the bank, whose father taught him to fish, has seen the situation deteriorate with each passing year. 'There used to be so many fish here, you could scoop them right out of the water, any kind of fish you can imagine. It was almost *too* easy, you didn't have to use bait. And ten years ago you could still catch good-sized fish here. Sea bass, that kind of thing. Now most of it is sardines, and you need good equipment if you're going to catch anything sizeable.' He lifts his lunchbox to show me his tackle: leaders and hooks of all shapes and sizes; heavy sinkers – for use in strong currents – ultra-thin lines – for deep water – feathered jigs – for long casts – hooks for sardines, hooks for sea bass, hooks for mackerel, lines for good weather, lines for bad weather, storms, rain, summer, autumn.

13

The regular fishermen all know each other, they pitch in whenever one of them hooks a fish that's hard to land, and newcomers receive wise advice. 'But if they're completely hopeless, we'd just as soon see them pack up and get out.' The favourite spots are close to the control towers: something interesting occasionally swims by there. But that's also where the angry men hang out, a group of embittered farmers who have failed to make it in the city; it's best to ignore them completely, otherwise they take out their rage on you. 'They have no manners,' the man from the bank complains. 'Not towards women either. Not even when they wear a veil. These days our city's full of country bumpkins!'

The evening rush hour has begun. From the streets to the north a steady flow of shop girls, workmen and office clerks shuffle tiredly towards the bridge. They descend to catch one of the ferries, or trundle on to one of the poorer neighbourhoods on the Muslim side. The sun is turning red behind the minarets. Wrapped up warmly against the wind, the pavement photographer walks back and forth dejectedly, his hood up, his dilapidated Polaroid camera clenched in his cold hands. He started this afternoon at one, has been standing here five hours, but with only two customers. 'I don't have time to talk to you now; six million, I can't live on that. I have to earn a couple of million more.'

Dozens of people are sitting on the steps close to the old city, waiting for the bus. A man strums a lute, the women have piled up their full baskets and carrier bags beside them, the children whine and hide their faces in their mothers' skirts. Everywhere there are little clusters of family bunched up together.

A little further along, lights blink on above the advertising boarding for Ramsey of London: a huge blond man in an armchair peers down at us questioningly; he's wearing a suit of orange velour and a white cravat, with a bookcase and lots of solid English woodwork in the background.

This is the moment when children begin appearing on the streets as well – the ones who sell tissues and adhesive bandages. There are the little carts of roasted chestnuts, porters with their rolls and baskets, the man with the big pile of pretzels balanced on his head, the shoeshine boys, the gamblers, the angry old woman, the lovers.

The pickpockets have spread out across the bridge. They calmly move along with the crowd, stroll about, come a little too close to a pair of tourists – 'Oh, excuse me!' – and in a twinkling it's happened again, like a cormorant jabbing a fish from the water, but faster. It's a relaxed and above all civilised activity, this professional fleecing of the handful of Europeans and Americans who venture out on to the bridge.

In the arcade, the voices are all ringing out together: the umbrella salesman, the man selling felt insoles, a ballpoint-pen vendor, a wallet pedlar, a battery man and a female beggar sporting an all too pitiful child and too many golden rings. The ironclad optimism of the lottery girl rises above it all: 'Create your own luck! Drawing on Saturday!' That's when the results of the big lotto will be announced. 'I've sold ninety tickets so far, I'm sure I'll make it to a hundred today,' she says cheerfully. The table in front of her is marked by a rigorous orderliness, all the tickets arranged neatly by category and bound with rubber bands. Her left eye is bruised and blackened. 'Today I know I'm going to make it.' Across from her a bookseller begins spreading out his wares on a few newspapers: several dozen dog-eared thrillers and novels, a couple of coffee-stained photo books. He will remain there deep into the night, waiting until after the steel shutters have all been lowered and the only passers-by are the riff-raff, calmly smoking one cigarette after the other.

Outside, meanwhile, the Wind of the Stars has come up. It is one of this city's stranger natural phenomena: great booming gusts of wind that come hurtling in off the river. Suddenly the waves have grown nasty little whitecaps, the ferries steam and puff to stay on course, on the terraces the place settings begin blowing off the tables, pavement signs

16

slam to the ground, sand bites the eyes. The man with the electric drill takes to his heels, the shoe-shine boys pack their things, the fishermen start reeling in their lines, but it is too late.

Atop the towers the huge plastic tulips crack loudly and fall one by one – it happens right before our eyes, we're nailed to the spot – those brightly coloured globes go flying across the bridge, dangerous buggers they are as well, so big that the photographer, the perfume vendor, the Spanish couple, the Americans, the pickpockets, the fisher-men, everyone on the bridge, we all have to run like mad not to be crushed by one of those ridicu-lous monster tulips.

Then the wind dies down.

II

The insole vendor began work at five thirty, when it was still dark outside. He rose from his bed while his room-mate was still asleep, got himself a bowl of soup in an early-morning café and now he's standing in the tunnel, waving his felt insoles. It is ten o'clock. The cold passes right through his reddish-brown coat and woollen cap, but worst of all are his teeth, which have been aching and terribly inflamed for the last few weeks. 'I need to buy myself antibiotics,' he says. 'But first I have to pay this friend of mine what I owe him, forty-five million, and I've only got till Friday.' He gets by these days on stale bread, but is no less optimistic for all that. Lots of soldiers have been crossing the bridge today and soldiers always have cold, sore feet from standing guard. What's more, even worse weather is on its way. He's already sold three pairs, bringing today's turnover to three million. With a little luck he'll make that twelve million by the time the day is over. 'I smoke a lot, that always helps to still the hunger.'

It's a fairly quiet morning. A group of about twenty fishermen are out on the bridge. The photographer got off to a late start, after working last night in another part of town. Fifteen million. The perfume vendor hasn't been around for days. The police commander – the bridge has its own police station – strolls back and forth magnanimously. 'Nothing to be done about it, there's no money crossing the bridge today.' 'Doesn't anyone ever jump over the railing?' 'No, they go to the other bridges, even to do that.'

I buy a couple of packs of Marlleak from Önder, one of the cigarette boys. 'What's wrong, are you getting bored?' He laughs. 'If it's shady, you name it and it happens here: muggings, pickpocketing, the gamblers over there even do each other in every once in a while.' He's seen plenty of shakedowns while working the tunnel: 'A group of about five guys supposedly starts fighting, then they draw a tourist into it and the rest is dead easy.' They all have their own method. 'There are a thousand surefire ways to lay your hands on money in Istanbul. And these guys are real specialists.' But surely no one falls for the old shell-game ploy any more? 'Don't underestimate our pickpockets, they're twice as professional as the ones where you come from. They're the best in Europe!'

The ferry boats stamp and hoot, always as though they were about to set sail for Odessa or Athens instead of on that little fifteen-minute crossing. The air is full of magpies, they crowd the trees around the palace, shooting back and forth in flocks across the ruined walls and forgotten domes, over the last remaining graves of what were once cemeteries.

In the tunnel the police commander trades jokes back and forth with Önder and his friends; the bridge is one great wickerwork of deals, averted gazes and right hands that have not the slightest idea what the left is up to. But suddenly there's an uproar in one of the side corridors: the little lookout boys have spotted a special police team and everyone sets off running. The vendors snatch up their assortments of cigarettes, mobile phones and toys, their pockets are bulging, the cardboard boxes that served as counters stand bare and helpless along the pavement. Eyes fixed innocently on the ceiling, the boys wait until the uniforms have passed.

Only the tea vendor remains calmly in place. His sole protection from the elements is a tattered tweed suit jacket, but he's the only one not bothered by the cold. When the weather is like this he enjoys a sort of immunity – the policemen, after all, drink his tea as well – and besides, everyone knows him, he's been here for the last four years. 'These are good days for business,' he says. Yet he is not a happy man. 'If I could earn five million a day in my own village, I'd go back tomorrow. But nothing ever really changes in my life and that's the way it's been for years.' Once the scare has blown over he gives the mobile-phone hawkers, those who spilled their tea amid all the chaos, new plastic cups: around here, the tea comes with a police-proof warranty.

The lives of the tea seller, the cigarette boys and the insole vendor are set against the backdrop of a remarkable corner of the globe, but precious little good that does them. 'There are places', the Russian poet Joseph Brodsky wrote, 'where history is inescapable, like a highway accident – places where geography provokes history. Such is Istanbul, alias Constantinople, alias Byzantium.' Islambol could be added to that list of aliases. Along with the Mansion of Bliss, the Sublime Port, the City of the Caliphate, the Gate to Happiness, the Eye of the World, the Passing Place of the Universe. The Greeks spoke simply of '*polis*' – 'the city' – there was no other. The city sprawls across the hills along the Bosporus, the busy strait between the Black Sea and the Mediterranean, at the exact spot where a river also empties itself. Across the mouth of that river, the Golden Horn, lies our bridge, but the place itself is much older. Long before the Christian era the ancient Greeks founded a colony, Byzantium, on this strategic peninsula. Later, Emperor Constantine the Great made it the new capital of the Roman Empire.

In the centuries that followed, this Nova Roma – or 'Constantinople' – grew to become the most important sea port in Europe, a vast treasure trove of the arts and classical learning, the living spirit of the Roman Empire and, at the same time, the heart of Orthodox Christianity. It ruled over an empire which, at its peak, stretched from the Alps and the Euphrates all the way to Gibraltar. In the sixth century Emperor Justinian had the Hagia Sophia built there, a cathedral with the largest dome the world had ever seen, seemingly suspended in air – an architectural tour de force that was only readily repeated in the nineteenth century. The Byzantine coin of the realm – the '*solidus*' – was the dollar of the early Middle Ages and retained that supremacy for seven centuries.

The Western European Crusaders were flabbergasted to find themselves entering a city which, according to one account from 1203, was filled with 'rich palaces and sublime churches', and where the splendid streets were peopled by merchants 'who look like princes'. Yet even then the Byzantine Empire had begun to disintegrate; from the inside out, due to the terror and plundering of these same Christian Crusaders, and from the outside in, due to attacks by so-called 'Turks', Muslim warriors descended from the nomads of Central Asia and feared everywhere for their speed, mobility and discipline.

The day on which the Osman Turks took the city, 29 May 1453, was known in the Christian West as 'the day the world ended'. It became a fault line between the two cultures: even today, we Westerners speak of 'the fall of Byzantium', while my acquaintances on the bridge, when we discuss history, always refer to 'the conquest of Istanbul'.

Blood ran through the gutters down to the Golden Horn, countless boys and girls ended up as slaves, houses and churches were plundered, down to the last nail. The bones of Saint Theodosia, honoured for seven centuries as mother and tutelary deity of the city, were taken from their golden casket and strewn about the muddy streets. According to the Venetian Nicolo Barbaro, who barely survived the bloodbath, hundreds of severed heads bobbed in the waters of the strait, in much the same way as a load of rotten melons would sometimes block the canals of his birthplace.

'Perhaps', writes Fernand Braudel in his *A History of Civilisations*, 'it has been the destiny of Islam to attract and use the primitive people who surround or cross its territory, but then to fall prey to their violent power. Ultimately, order is restored and wounds are healed. The successful primitive warrior is tamed by the all-powerful urban life of Islam.'

That is how it happened with our city as well.

When Sultan Mehmet II, the Ottoman commander, took Constantinople he was twenty-two years old. His cruelty was legendary – upon discovering that a cucumber was missing from his beloved gardens, he had all his gardeners disembowelled in order to locate the guilty party. At the same time he was an unsurpassed strategist who spoke numerous languages and looked far beyond the horizons of his own territory. His qualities as an administrator came as something of a surprise: within a few decades he had founded a new empire upon the ruins of old Byzantium. The city was entirely rebuilt. Instead of a sealed fortress town full of ancient treasures, it became a dynamic port and trading town, a place of refuge for Spanish and Portuguese Jews and other persecuted groups, as well as a centre of government for a religiously inspired world empire in the making.

'I know of no state more fortunate than this; it has been bestowed with all God's gifts,' another Venetian visitor wrote in 1528. 'It masters the arts of both war and peace, and is rich in gold, people, ships and obedience.' The city's population in those days was every bit as large as that of Paris. A drawing by Melchior Lorich dating from 1560 shows the Golden Horn so full of sails, masts and rigging that the viewer can barely see the water. All the empire's trade came through the capital, by way of overland routes from Poland and Syria, and the sea routes from Venice, Marseilles and the Crimea. Caravans of up to two thousand camels and mules arrived at least once a month from Persia, the terminus of a trade route that ran all the way to China.

The Ottomans attached great importance to serenity and immutability. In the few views of the city that remain from that era it is almost impossible to determine whether the scene is from the sixteenth or the eighteenth century: the palaces, gates, minarets, graveyards, merchants, dogs and beggars looked very much the same in 1750 as they had in 1550. It is only by virtue of the British, Venetian and Dutch ships one sees in the views of the Golden Horn that one can more or less date such paintings and etchings. The rest creates an illusion of indestructible certainty and continuity.

In actual fact, however, the city lived in a permanent state of flux; nowhere else on earth did the razing, wrecking and reconstruction go on as busily as in Istanbul. The French humanist and man of science Pierre Gilles, who made an inventory between 1544 and 1547, could find almost nothing remaining of the former Byzantine and Roman Istanbul. After less than a century of Ottoman construction, destruction and replacement, virtually all the forums, porticoes and other Roman architectural wonders had vanished. 'And had I not seen so many ruined churches and palaces and their foundations, since filled with Mahometan buildings . . . I would not so easily have guessed what destruction the Turks had accomplished since they took the city.'

On a regular basis, entire neighbourhoods burnt to the ground. In most other major European cities all-wooden houses had long been banned for precisely that reason. Here the wooden house – usually painted a rusty red – formed the core of family life. Wood was plentiful, from the forests surrounding the city, and could be used to build magnificent houses quickly and inexpensively. What's more, such houses were earthquake-resistant. For this golden city, after all, had one handicap: far below the surface it lay on a fault line as well, and tremors and quakes were commonplace.

At heart, old Stamboul remained a huddle of villages. Daily life took place largely within the neighbourhood, within the fixed triangle of home, market and mosque (or church, in the Christian neighbourhoods, or synagogue in the Jewish ones). Each neighbourhood had its own specific character – Islamic, Armenian, Jewish, Greek, Western – that led foreign visitors passing through the district gates to feel as though they were walking from one culture into the next.

In much the same way, the rest of Ottoman society – both religious and worldly – was run according to clear lines of demarcation. Within those limits rules were relatively lax, but major problems arose whenever a border was violated. The wealthier households had strictly separated spaces for the public and the private, for men and women, for guests and family, for senior and less senior servants, for older and younger children.

The man of the house was lord over all; he was allowed to have four wives and as many slave girls as he liked – but it was considered unseemly for him to interfere with matters in the women's section, which was run by his mother and his first wife. The women often lived together in relative harmony. And often enough as well the atmosphere was one of intense jealousy. 'The constant tension in our house made even the simplest of ceremonies an event that caused an almost physical pain,' wrote Halide Edib, one of the city's first feminists and daughter of one of the sultan's chamberlains, in her memoirs. 'The women's rooms were arranged opposite each other, and my father visited each of them in turn. . . .'

The strict divisions continued on the street as well: the mosque for religious meetings, the coffee-house for secular matters; fixed walking days for Muslim women, other fixed walking days for Muslim men; one side of the river for the general populace, the other for Westerners; districts here for the Muslims, that neighbourhood over there for the

Greeks, another for the Jews, a little further along the Armenians.

In this way a society could arise that consisted of communities that worked and did business together, but were otherwise imprisoned in their own compartments of neighbourhood, house, family, gender, rank and standing. When the first railways were built some Jewish workers were unable to take part because they still spoke only Ladino, a kind of Castilian: they could not express themselves in the language of the city in which they lived, three hundred years after their ancestors had fled there from Spain.

Let us take another look over the shoulder of Edmondo de Amicis, there amid his crowd on the bridge in 1878:

> Before you even have time to turn back you find yourself among a group of Persians with their tall, pointed Astrakhan caps, and when they have passed you see before you a Jew in a long yellow robe open at the sides; a heathen woman with her hair undone, carrying a child in a sling on her back; a Catholic priest with his walking stick and prayer book, while out of the midst of a tumultuous group of Turks, Greeks and Armenians a huge eunuch on horseback shouts, 'Stand aside!'

What de Amicis saw streaming past were the inhabitants of what was perhaps the most multicultural city of all time: a bizarre hotchpotch of Europe and Asia, of West and East. At the same time he was struck by the fact that 'all these souls meet and pass by without paying each other heed', that all of these peoples and cultures inhabited worlds of their own.

The city's tolerance depended on looking the other way; contact with those other worlds was devoid of all curiosity. The Ottomans did not maintain permanent envoys to foreign capitals, for they found that unnecessarily expensive and inconvenient. Everyone was welcome, but it was strictly a one-way street. The capital of the world was, in the final account, concerned only with itself.

Just outside the arcade of shops beside the bridge, beneath the arches of a large office building, one finds a narrow alleyway. There, amid boxes of shadowy merchandise, a handful of low stools and orange crates, is the sheltered spot where the insole vendor and his friends take a break, drink a glass of tea, eat a sardine, smoke a cigarette. 'We usually talk about day-to-day things: money problems, the news on the radio, the police, the weather,' he says. 'Your son gets married, the bride's parents are putting up a lot of money, you've got almost nothing, how do you solve that? That kind of thing.'

The insole vendor's daily budget – his name is actually Ali Özbagriaçik – is allotted as follows: morning soup: one million; cigarettes: two million; tea: one million; dinner at a roadside stand: two million; a bed at the boarding house: three million. His friends, however, say that he has failed to mention his final purchase of the day: before going to sleep he drinks a bottle of red wine, the cheapest sort, the kind they refer to around here as 'dog-killer'. Lots of the local merchants drink it. Two million. Bringing us to a total of eleven million. And he usually slips his son a little money as well. His daily turnover is somewhere between twelve and sixteen million. 'I work every day, including weekends. If I skipped a day, I couldn't support myself.'

On the bridge, sickness is out of the question, hospitals beyond the realm of possibility. In this world physical ailments precipitate a twin disaster: the money needed for doctors and medicine, plus revenues lost. 'I'm always healthy, God be praised,' the boys on the bridge will tell you. Önder: 'Everyone I know is as poor as a rat, so how could they take care of me? That's the way it is. My friend, I'm not telling you anything other than the way it is.'

That is why all complaints here, from rotting gums to burning stomach acid, are blasted with antibiotics. 'I've lost almost all my hair,' the insole

30

vendor says. 'So if my head gets cold, my teeth start hurting. And then it spreads to my throat.' This problem, too, is one he will treat with a few light-blue pills, as soon as he has a little money to spare.

He was born in 1951, in Izmir, and his family was never anything but poor. As a little boy he used to sell socks, paper handkerchiefs, matches, pens, that kind of thing. In the 1960s he found work in a textile plant – those were the fat years: Sundays off, even holidays. From his inside pocket he produces an ID card with a picture of a handsome fellow, black moustache, flashing eyes. 'That was back when I worked at the factory, I was married, had three children; life was a piece of cake, and I could buy all the bread I wanted.'

Ten years after that picture was taken his brother talked him into moving to Istanbul, to open a clothing shop. They put all their money into it, just before the big economic crash. The brothers went bankrupt, he was no longer able to support his family, his wife sued for divorce, he moved into a shared room in a cheap boarding house, and for the last few years this is where he's been peddling his wares. 'I don't have a future. This is all I think about at night. I had a steady job for twenty-one years; if I could find another one and keep it for three years I could collect a state pension. But who's going to take on a fifty-five-year-old man?'

There were six of them on the bridge at first, six street merchants, and they formed a pact of friendship. 'We sold insoles, toys, sunglasses, hats, all kinds of things. If we happened to be selling the same merchandise, because we'd found out about a big shipment somewhere, we always moved off to different parts of the bridge. And if one of us became ill or was robbed, we helped each other out financially.' The alliance remained in force for five years, then it fell apart. Two of the men went back to their villages, the rest found work elsewhere. He and the bookseller are the only ones left. 'We're still friends, we do whatever we can.'

I ask him what the Ali of 1984 would have thought of the Ali of 2006. He is quiet for a moment. 'So many years have gone by since then, entire lifetimes. You grow accustomed to your own face in the mirror, I'm still the same man I was then. You think: if only I had stayed on at the factory for another three years, if only I hadn't gone to Istanbul . . . Take my situation now, for example. My teeth and my throat hurt, and I can't afford to buy medicine, so what am I supposed to do? But listen, no one gets to determine his own fate. The most important thing is your dignity, that's one thing you must never give up.'

Talk turns to the world of Mammon that surrounds his poverty, to the world of advertising and the glossy magazines with which one is confronted all day, every day, even on the bridge. The way the insole vendor looks at it, most of the well-to-do, respectably dressed people who walk by him in the course of a day are rather like robots. 'Rich people don't tend to help poor people like us. They have no feelings. You never see a rich person coming over to buy something. Poor people are the only ones willing to give me a little trade, they still feel love and other emotions.'

One of this year's best-sellers is a book called *The Third World War*. The story is set in the year 2010 and tells of a vengeful Turkey that, fed up with repeated humiliations, finally declares war on the decadent European Union and, together with Russia, marches on Berlin, Vienna and Paris. Is he familiar with that kind of rage? 'Being angry doesn't change anything. Someone else might have a Mercedes and a beautiful wife, and I might wish I had those myself, but it will never happen. All I can do is face up to that. I do my best to cope with the way things are. That's why I have no more expectations.'

What bothers him, however, is that he can't help his children financially at this point. When his youngest son goes out with schoolmates and the others all buy a bottle of cola, his son can't join them. That rankles, and he keeps coming back to it. 'I don't want that to happen to him. So I give him a little spending money.' The insole vendor has almost no contact with his oldest son. 'They say he's doing well. But he doesn't talk to me any more; you know, we were separated for so long. A few months ago I saw him with his brother, looking at me, they were way over there while I was selling my things in front of the tunnel. My boys. They didn't come over, they didn't say a word, they just stood there looking at me.'

Gradually I become better acquainted with both city and bridge. My interpreter is a young student, a friendly beanpole of a boy by the name of Mehmet Onur, which could be translated as 'Mehmet Honour'. One could not, under these conditions, ask for better company. Over coffee at the little tables at the Galata Café, our civilisations clash on a daily basis. 'In Western Europe, freedom of speech is considered a fundamental civil right,' I remark, muttering over a newspaper article about yet another Turkish writer dragged before a court for no good reason.

'But if, for example, someone writes that Kemal Atatürk's mother was a tart,' Onur objects, 'then such disrespect cannot go unpunished, can it?'

'But it's not a matter for the criminal courts,' I say. 'What you have to do is fire back a reply. Fight words with words.' Onur shakes his head in disbelief.

Slowly I start to feel that I have re-entered the world of our grandparents and great-grandparents, a way of life that revolves around family ties, honour and personal dignity; a society where, in the long run, a person can rely only on the support of his family, his neighbours and the occasional friend.

'Is the insole vendor exaggerating when he says he has no expectations?' I ask Onur.

'Oh, no,' he says. 'What he tells you is a realistic assessment of his situation. If he doesn't care for himself, no one else will.'

'But did his wife really leave him because he had no money?'

'Surveys in Turkey show that things like that happen fairly often. When marriages break up here, it's often for economic reasons. When a man can no longer support a woman and her children, who else will? Women in those situations often have no choice but to go back to their families.'

We talk about Önder, whose father can't find a job; he has to support a family of eight with the cigarettes he and his brother manage to hawk. His cheery disposition seems unsinkable, but it's clear that at times he barely gets by. 'A family like that', Onur says, 'must be on the verge of returning to the mother's village; that's the only place they can still find help.'

The economy of the bridge, therefore, is an economy of spare change and after a few days that also has come to seem normal to me. Standing beside the insole vendor, we wait half an hour for a tiny transaction to take place: three million, the equivalent of one euro and fifty cents, but there is no one here who would turn up his nose at that. The official statistics leave no room for misunderstanding: the 'poverty line' – the minimum income required to meet the daily basic needs of a family of four – is 1,818 million per month; the 'subsistence line' for the same family – the minimum required for adequate nutrition – is 558 million. The legal net minimum wage, however, is 380 million per month. The average Turkish family can live on that for exactly twenty days, but only if they don't spend a penny on anything but food. With the exception of the pickpockets and the fishermen, I know of nobody on the bridge who earns more than a subsistence income. Most of them make do with far less.

And then there is the perpetual uncertainty. Stability is unknown – even the slightest waver in the city's economy is felt immediately on the bridge. Everyone is here for more or less the same reason: a poor mountain village that barely survived the years, yet survived nonetheless; families in which, thanks to improved health care, more and more children live beyond infancy; a stony soil that cannot feed all the mouths depending on it; children who are finally sent off to seek their fortune in the big city.

The tea vendor, for example, comes from a village very like that of the perfume salesman, close to the Iranian border. His family still lives there. He has been away from home for years, and visits his wife and children every three months: a twenty-four-hour journey each way. 'I work here for them, only for them. If you went to my village you'd be amazed. We're all normal people, just like you, and you'd be amazed to see how those normal people have to live. We've all experienced hunger, and great hunger at that!' He waves his hand to indicate the people around him. 'Everyone here, almost all of us come from the back of beyond, from south-eastern Turkey. But there's nothing there for us. Unless you want to go into the mountains, to join the terrorists. If you don't want to do that, you have no choice but to make the best of things here, to sell tea, or flog pirated CDs, or shift stolen mobile phones, or sell fake perfume to people like you – yeah, watch out for that rubbish, it can make you go blind. You think we do this because we like it?'

The waiter at Galata Café: 'My grandfather died last month. He barely knew what money was. He was over a hundred, a shepherd, he spent his whole life wandering the mountains with his sheep. Except for the last few years, then all he did was go to the mosque to pray.' His grandfather lived five minutes from the Iranian border. 'We know the mountains well, we know where it's safe and what

37

to do when war breaks out and the planes start flying over. Surviving is one thing we're good at. But making sure there's enough to eat . . . ' He left for Istanbul in 2004, after the latest war had put an effective end to all commerce in his village. New arrivals in the big city always speak of 'a cousin' or 'a neighbour from my village' who assists them. And if you don't know anyone in town there are always people from your village or region who will show you the ropes – because they're a kind of family too. Ask the insole vendor and the bookseller why they're friends and they'll laugh a little – the insole vendor has read maybe three books in his whole life – but then they'll say: 'Both of us come from Izmir and our children live far away.' That's how one gets by.

One rainy Saturday afternoon the bookseller, who sees and hears everything, gave Onur and myself a short lecture on the sociology of the bridge. What he described amounted to a kind of economic compartmentalisation. The fishmongers, for example, all hail from the eastern city of Erzincan. Most of the professional anglers come from Trabzon, on the Black Sea. The rods and tackle, on the other hand, are sold generally by immigrants from Kastamonu and there's no getting around them. And if you're Kurdish there is no sense in trying to rent a space and fry fish, for that monopoly is in the hands of another group. On the other hand, though, you could move into the cigarette trade immediately. 'We are one family,' the cigarette boys say. 'When the police start hassling people we always help each other, we drag each other's wares along, hide other people's things for them; if we didn't do that we'd all be wiped off the street.'

Countless tightly knit immigrant communities exist in this way, all of them operating in isolation from the others and within the strict borders allotted them. Traditionally, the city has always been an amalgam of more or less closed urban villages and beneath the surface – and certainly among immigrants – those old demarcations continue to play a role. There are still, for example, two Armenian hospitals in Istanbul and eighteen Armenian schools. 'There are clubs for immigrants everywhere, tiny groups no one's ever heard of. And they all have their own newspaper,' says the bookseller. 'There are ten million people in this city, after all, which means there's a market for everything.'

The divisions are visible along political lines as well – on and below the bridge, for example, the Kurds and the nationalists live in a state of deft mutual avoidance. The bookseller is a liberal Muslim, an Alawite. Together, the umbrella sales-men form a fledgling socialist enclave. The charming man who sells umbrellas in the arcade, opposite the lottery-ticket girl and the gun shop, was once a typical *soixante-huitard*. He told me about his heroes, Fidel Castro and Che Guevara, and how hard young people worked back then to build a better world. They craved the same things as their contemporaries in Western Europe: workers' rights, free medical care, better schools, a more prominent role for culture. 'But now socialism is melting away before my eyes, that's my great sorrow. People are retreating into the old ways, the social economy is disappearing. The sort of young people who used to become Marxists are now becoming Islamists.'

He finally ended up on the bridge. 'Sunglasses in the summertime, umbrellas all winter long, that's the way it's been for twenty-eight years now. A lifetime has gone by before you know it and what can anyone do about that?'

Orhan Pamuk, the urban chronicler who ultimately won the Nobel Prize for Literature, once provided a clear-eyed description of workaday existence in a poor, undemocratic, often Muslim country. Those who lead such an existence know that they have been condemned to a hard, brief and usually insignificant life. They also know that, to a certain extent, their poverty is down to their own foolish-ness and faults, or those of their parents or grandparents. As a result their private lives are almost permanently in a state of grim derangement, something one rarely reads about in travel literature or political analyses.

'The Western world is scarcely aware of this overwhelming feeling of humiliation that is experienced by most of the world's population; it is a feeling that people have to try to overcome without losing their common sense, and without being seduced by terrorists, extreme nationalists or fundamentalists.'

Is there any way out? Almost everyone on the bridge finds themselves suspended between two worlds and all have dreamed of making that great leap forward. 'Of course I'd like to go to Europe, we all want to do that, but have you ever tried getting in?' the tea vendor complains. 'Who doesn't think about that?' the insole vendor says. 'But what do I have left? I can't even afford a passport.' 'If I could get away from here, I wouldn't know where to go,' says the waiter. 'With all the competition from Asia, you can't earn a decent living in a factory any more.' The perfume salesman says dreamily, 'There's one country over there, another country over here, but otherwise it's all just people, normal people, the only difference is the language.'

The cigarette boys revere a shining example of their own, one of Önder's uncles who found a way to get into Belgium, earned lots of money and ultimately married a blonde woman. 'My God, Europe, we'd love to go there. There's plenty of money there, you can do whatever you want, the people respect each other.' I do my best to put a little water in the wine, but they insist that Europe's problems are nothing compared with theirs. 'I'm not interested in luxury,' Önder says. 'Rich people's lives aren't any better than poor people's. I just want to take care of my family. And of myself. And of course I want to get married. To a beautiful foreign woman. A blonde Belgian . . .'

'If you wait ten years or so, the borders will be opened anyway,' I suggest.

'But I'll be old by then! Perhaps even dead!'

Önder is one of the few who has ever really tried properly to get away. One night he and a couple of friends hid in a container bound for Europe. They'd prepared themselves well for the journey: they had bread, water, warm clothing, plastic rubbish bags to pull over their heads if they went through an infrared detector; they'd thought of almost everything. Except tranquillisers. One of the boys was a real nervous wreck. Just when their container was passing through the infrared port – they were all sitting in the dark with bags over their heads – he had to go and have a nervous attack. 'He started screaming and shaking all over; I felt bad luck coming our way and there they were, the doors opened and police-men with dogs were everywhere. They dragged us out of the container, beat the living daylights out of us and kept shouting: "Why are you trying to get out of our country? Isn't our country good enough for you?"' Önder was fifteen at the time. The boys were sent back to their families and that was that. 'Later, one of my friends had another go. They beat him so badly that he was almost unrecognisable. No, we won't try that one again.'

The umbrella salesman did his best to get out too, years and years ago. In 1992, with the help of a cousin who lived there, he tried to emigrate to England. His European sojourn lasted a full three hours. He had borrowed some money and bought a Turkish Airlines ticket to London, but got no further than immigration at Heathrow. 'I shouted that they would arrest me as soon as I got back to Turkey, that I was a political refugee, that I would never be able to pay back the money I'd borrowed for that ticket!' They sent him home on the same plane. 'Deal with your problems in your own country, not here,' they told him. 'I felt like a chunk of meat that had been tossed to the wolves.' Fourteen years later he still flies into a rage whenever he talks about it, as though it had happened just last month. 'I had to work like mad for ages just to pay back that ticket. And if I hadn't repaid what I owed, I wouldn't be here to talk about it, believe me.'

He still dreams of taking legal action against England. 'Yes, why not? Against the whole country! I don't speak a word of English, I don't

43

have any money, but some day I'll get them!' How, we wondered, was he going to do that? 'I'll drag them into court. That's right, I read about that somewhere, you can do that!'

III

In my bookcase I have a seventeenth-century
volume inherited from a dear relative, a leather-
bound copy of *19 jaarige lant-reyse* ('A 19-years'
Journey') by Willem Lithgouw, printed in
Amsterdam *'behinde the Appelmarckt'* in the year
1653. The truth of the matter was that it was one of
those things I had never got around to reading,
more a precious curio than a book. But at one point
during my forays on the bridge, it occurred to me
that Lithgouw, an old salt who had seen most of the
Near East, might have had a few things to say about
Istanbul as well.

That proved to be very much the case; along
with a French naval officer, in fact, Lithgouw had
once set out to rescue 'a Christian soul' from
Turkish slavery, all 'to render service unto God'.
This 'Christian soul', they decided, was to be a
'pure Virgine or Widowe'. Lithgouw's account
describes in detail how the two men went to the
'Weibermarkt' and inspected one 'staerk naked'
soul after another. The virgins were way beyond
their means, so finally they decided to purchase a
Dalmatian widow for thirty-six ducats. They rowed

across the river and rented a room for her on the far shore; freedom beckoned. The next morning, however, Lithgouw discovered to his great chagrin that this 'old lecher', this French 'Papist', had 'lain' with their widow all that night and that he was even planning to sell her on to someone else. By threatening to involve the French envoy in Istanbul, Lithgouw finally freed the widow, found her a job in a Greek taverna – for which he received from her, he claimed, nothing but 'blessings and signs of utmoste gratitude' – and then went on his way with a clear conscience. A typical Dutchman, however, he pauses in his narrative to remind the reader that this 'night of fornication' cost the luckless Frenchie no less than thiirty-six ducats.

More than two centuries later the French writer Pierre Loti tried in somewhat more subtle fashion to save another woman's soul from 'Turkish lust' (throughout the nineteenth century *The Lustful Turk* was an extremely popular piece of pornographic literature); he, of course, had in mind the same thing as his countryman of 1653. In the novel *Aziyadé,* which he wrote years afterwards, he described an amorous adventure with an Ottoman woman, which his letters and journals show actually took place.

Officer Loti's frigate docks at Saloniki. As he is walking through the old Turkish neighbourhoods, deep in thought, he is suddenly struck by a pair of big green eyes staring at him from behind a white veil and a set of heavy iron bars. The eyes, as it turns out, belong to an eighteen-year-old girl, the fourth wife of a wealthy merchant. A romance begins, Loti succeeds in having her smuggled out of the harem on a few occasions and finally, amid the French and German warships, on the cushions of a softly rocking boat, they make love.

The merchant moves to Istanbul, Loti succeeds in tracking down his paramour – but only after having numerous other romantic encounters in the local graveyards – and the affair resumes. Loti now has a little house of his own and night after night Aziyadé – whose name in real life was Hakidjé – succeeds in slipping out of the harem. The merchant, after all, is always off travelling, and Loti and the girl share a few blissful months together.

In March 1877 the dreaded moment arrives: it is time for Loti's ship to return home. Aziyadé, broken-hearted, organises a farewell party with a few friends. She is lovelier than ever: a waistcoat of purple silk, wide trousers of yellow silk, a gauzy blouse embroidered with silver, her hair in thick brown plaits, her lips red, her arms the colour of amber and no veil – everyone assumes she must be Armenian.

By the next morning she has thrown all caution to the wind. She walks openly with him through the city, to the waterfront to say goodbye. Loti steps into the sloop, the wheels of her carriage rattle away. 'And a mad urge came over me to run off after that carriage, to take my dearest one in my arms, to hold her tight as we loved each other one last time with all the strength in our hearts, and to never let each other go until the hour of death.'

With the story of his romance in the Great Cemetery Loti achieved international fame. After his departure the real Aziyadé was betrayed and finally locked away by her cuckolded husband. After a year of misery she died, but Loti heard of her death only ten years later. Material enough for yet another best-seller.

In all these Western accounts the north bank of the estuary was always the place of refuge, the better world. In the fourteenth century, after all manner of military and diplomatic clashes, merchants from Genoa were given permission to set up their own trade mission there. The houses and buildings of the free port were arranged against the hillside in the form of an amphitheatre, with a fortified tower at the top.

The district was called Galata and the entire area was referred to as Pera – Greek for 'outside'. The Genoans were allowed to run it as though it were their own. The Venetians soon followed, then came the French, the British and the Dutch. Bit by bit, all these delegations began to resemble something like foreign royal households, complete with pages, ladies-in-waiting, palaces and country estates: the Palazzo di Venetia, the Palais de France, the British Palace, Palais d'Hollande.

The Ottomans, with their tolerance and openness towards merchants, immigrants, Christians and other minorities, were heirs to the old Roman imperial tradition. After the sacking of 1453, of course, the city was given a new name: Islambol, meaning 'where Islam blossoms bountifully'. The Hagia Sophia was converted into a mosque and from 1517 on the Ottoman sultan was even given the title 'Caliph of All Believers'. At the same time, however, these rulers spoke of themselves as 'conquerors of the world', yet the city was to be 'a place of refuge for the whole world'. An imperial capital, as they were well aware, must always reflect the diversity of the empire.

From a census conducted in 1477, less than twenty-five years, in other words, after 'the blackest day in history', it appears that more than a third of the city's houses were again occupied by Greeks, one-fifth by Jews and one-seventh by other non-Muslims. In a charter drawn up by Mehmet II the sultan guaranteed Christians and Jews full religious freedom – the only exception being a ban on the ringing of church bells. His elite troops, the janissaries, were purposely recruited from Christian families. The boys were taken away from their parents at an early age, circumcised and converted to Islam, then trained to perform the most demanding military tasks and to occupy the highest ranks. Yet Istanbul's minorities were never forced to adopt the dominant religion, a situation unique in the Europe of that day.

This tolerance, however, was not entirely uncontroversial. From the seventeenth century onwards there arose, just as among Christians in Northern Europe, a movement that wanted to return to the 'pure' faith. Medina, not Rome, was to be the reference point for the city. In certain districts, fundamentalist clerics gained an increasingly firm foothold: dancing, the wearing of silk, the enjoyment of coffee and tobacco were all to be banned.

Although the Golden Horn appeared to be nothing more than the mouth of a river, Edmondo de Amicis claimed that in reality it constituted an ocean.

The tidings from Europe, which pass through Galata and Pera quickly, clearly and accurately and are the subject of discussion there, reach the far shore only in mutilated form, fragmented as a distant echo; the fame of the greatest men and affairs of the West is blocked by that stretch of water, as by an impassable wall; and across that bridge, traversed by hundreds of thousands of people each day, not one idea crosses in a decade.

Many residents of the old city, in turn, saw Pera as the gates of hell, a place where few women wore veils and where no respectable person would be seen after dark. 'When a man goes to Pera, everyone knows what he is looking for,' a prominent Turkish reformer spat at the French ambassador in the late nineteenth century. 'You have not become acquainted with the spirit of the Ottoman state, or even the living conditions in Istanbul. Pera is an isthmus between Europe and the Muslim world. From there you view Istanbul through a pair of opera glasses.'

Travellers' accounts invariably mention the darkness in which traditional Istanbul veiled itself after sundown, while in Pera gas lamps were lit and remained so until dawn. 'In Galata, that city big / Each barrel holds a thousand swigs,' ran a well-known nineteenth-century rhyme. Countless stray dogs ran amok along with the rest, all night long, barking and howling so fearfully that one traveller in 1859 wrote, 'The screeching, howling, baying, growling and snarling melted into one unwavering and constant din.'

Yet the old city's interest in the Westerners' world grew and, as the once tightly knit neighbourhood communities began to dissolve, more and more of the city's inhabitants broke out of the traditional Ottoman seclusion. Pera, long since the district for things foreign and new, now became

51

the outpost for the free and modern life that awaited one and all. The 'Grand' and 'Little' cemeteries became favourite spots for evening strolls and daring encounters – Pierre Loti even maintained a pied-à-terre near the Grand Champ du Mort. The Metropolitan Railway of Istanbul was established around this time as well, opening the first and shortest underground railway line in Europe – the 'Tünel', a line precisely 500 metres long running between the bridge and La Grande Rue in Pera. Bank after bank, department store after department store arose, huge neo-baroque buildings like those going up all over Europe, but which in Istanbul generated unparalleled excitement.

In 1840 Gérard de Nerval perused the district's shops: beautiful display windows, jewellers, fashionable clothing, lingerie and patisseries, just like in Paris. He entered a café: on the reading tables lay newspapers with titles like *Journal de Constantinople*, *Echo de Smyrne*, *Portefolio Maltais*, *Courier d'Athènes*, *Moniteur Ottoman*. The British had a local cricket club. An Italian circus came through, and a French theatre troupe, and a man who had himself shot from a cannon.

The Ottoman middle classes became increasingly enchanted with the novelties to be seen on the far shore. Entire Ottoman families filed through its streets, not for religious reasons but simply to witness and partake of this fascinating new life. To shop on Pera's Grande Rue was, in the words of city historian Ekrim Isin, rather like taking 'a stroll through a museum of European civilisation'. Almost every travel account made note of the enormous 'half-Turkish, half-European crowd', which crossed the bridge each afternoon to throng the main shopping street in Pera. But it all became too much, even for the 'modern' sultan of that day: he passed a decree banning Turkish women from entering European shops. They were allowed only to stand and dream before the display window.

The slave trade still existed, but the actual market itself was closed in 1847 as the site of what the sultan called a 'shameful and barbaric practice'. When this same sultan discovered that his favourite wife had taken a lover, the man was not stuffed into a cannon and blasted to smithereens as he would have been in the past, but simply banned from the city. A 'modern' outlook raised one's status and the better-situated Ottomans came flocking into Pera to buy Western furniture, for example, or a piano – not so much to play Schubert upon, but mostly as a mark of distinction: 'We are Western and modern' was what the piano symbolised. All finery, of course, had to come from abroad as well. Turkey's traditional production of its own silk and embroidery was out of fashion, forgotten, passé. The citizens of this city wanted something else – without knowing precisely what.

★

It was only obvious, therefore, that the ocean between the old and the modern city should now be bridged by physical means as well. Plans to that effect had existed for centuries. Letters to the sultan from Leonardo da Vinci and Michelangelo have even been discovered containing proposals for a bridge across the Golden Horn. But the rulers saw no need. It was, in fact, a textbook example of what historians sometimes refer to as the 'economics of stagnation': inaction had – and has – not only disadvantages, but obvious advantages as well.

What's more, the city's ferrymen constituted a remarkable guild. During the soothing calm of the crossing they often served – if only for the space of fifteen minutes – as confidants to the townspeople. They were the oral historians of the city, amateur philosophers, accomplices in escapades and dubious adventures. Those crossings were frequently imbued with a rare restfulness and provided a moment of détente for everyone involved. Even without a bridge, Istanbul was city enough.

In the end, however, a total of five Galata Bridges were built – not counting the one Sultan Mehmet II assembled during his conquest of the city in 1453, when he had thousands of slaves and soldiers drag eighty ships over Galata Hill, the rowers seated and rowing as hard as they could over dry land. Five bridges, therefore: two wooden ones built in 1845 and 1863, two iron ones from 1875 and 1912, and a concrete one built in 1994.

The first known photograph of a bridge here dates from 1855 or 1856 and was taken by an Englishman by the name of Robertson. In it we see a pontoon bridge, with the contours of two fairly pronounced arched constructions at either end to allow smaller vessels to pass. From the very start, this 'bridge of boats' as the nineteenth-century writer and journalist Théophile Gautier dubbed it, was a city in itself. The tollage rates show us the types of vehicle that crossed it: horses carrying loads and horses without, donkeys and water buffalo, phaetons and carriages pulled by a single horse, porters, handcarts with and without passengers, sheep, goats, ox carts and of course a steady flow of pedestrians. In October 1855, during the Crimean War, Lady Edmund Hornby, wife of the British consul, wrote vividly of the throngs of British and French soldiers on the bridge. The street vendors quickly adapted to the new situation with cries of 'Johnny!' and '*Dis donc!*', but when a Muslim woman passed in a carriage the Europeans often peered in much too rudely, and many a eunuch was constrained to crack his whip in warning.

Less than twenty years after it was built this first bridge was already rotten and dilapidated. The second bridge, from 1863, barely lasted a decade. As early as 1872 a contract had been signed for a new bridge; this time it was to be a construction with twenty-four pontoons. The central sections could open and close like a pair of floating casement doors, allowing larger ships through. And in those days the water of the Golden Horn was still so clean that dressing cubicles for bathers were erected on the pontoons.

In 1878 a row of coffeehouses, restaurants and shops was added beneath the bridge: this combination of elevated roadway and underhanging entertainment district would characterise all Galata Bridges that followed. The crowds were enormous, the pavements narrow, and the carts and carriages did not drive on the left or the right, as they did almost everywhere else in the world, but raced across willy-nilly, with porters, barrowmen, street vendors and countless pedestrians worming their way between them. This was the bridge as described by de Amicis, as depicted by a host of Romantic Western painters and, from a distance one early morning, as beheld by the main character of Virginia Woolf's *Orlando*: 'There the Galata Bridge; there the green turbaned pilgrims without eyes or noses, begging alms; there the pariah dogs picking up offal; there the shawled women; there the innumerable donkeys; there men on horses carrying long poles.'

I discovered a column written long ago by Istanbul-chronicler Refik Halid Karay, in which he reminisces about the third Galata Bridge. The thing, he said, was 'tossed together from planks and wreckage', the huge nails holding the sleepers in place fell out regularly and 'many people stumbled, fell, were hurt and maimed'. The Ministry of the Navy was responsible for the bridge's maintenance, 'but in those days the Ministry was a den of thieves'.

The iron balustrades were mounted so shakily that it was ill advised to lean against them. One day a group of about forty men – most just in from the Turkish countryside – were leaning unsuspectingly over the balustrade, watching the fishermen in their boats. When the railing collapsed, Karay claimed, about twenty of the men drowned. 'But it wasn't reported in the papers.'

Meanwhile, under the bridge where the water is deepest, the remains of a thousand years of city piled up slowly. Orhan Pamuk has written a dazzling fantasy about that, but the other urban observers were no slouches either. At the bottom of the Horn one found not only the usual bottles, pistols, reaping hooks, harnesses, rotten rowing boats, imperial coins, pilgrims' insignias and Byzantine piss-pots, but also, for example, the municipal ferry that disappeared without a trace one morning. As it turned out, the ship had taken on water during the night and sunk like a brick to the bottom – that particular bit of wreckage, though, was later salvaged. And somewhere on the muddy bed must also lie the opulent carriage that once belonged to Mayor Mazhar Pasha's son-in-law, who, on another dark night, raced at breakneck speed right off the end of the opened bridge: coach, coachman and son-in-law were never seen again.

Throughout all those centuries the Ottoman Empire had two faces. It had a sleepiness, a lethargy, but there were always periods of great dynamism. The public facilities of seventeenth- and eighteenth-century Istanbul, for example, were excellent, at least by contemporary standards. The outstanding Roman and Byzantine system of water towers and aqueducts was in constant use, while the food supply was secured – in accordance with Roman tradition as well – by means of huge strategic stockpiles of grain that could be drawn on in emergencies to keep prices down and avoid rioting.

The Ottoman state archives, Braudel writes, reveal 'the workings of a multifarious, painstaking, advanced and authoritarian bureaucracy which was able to compile a detailed census, devise a coherent administrative policy, amass huge reserves of gold and silver, and systematically colonise the Balkans, the bastion of the empire against Europe, by settling nomads there . . . It all seems curiously modern.' The Ottomans were also skilled in adapting to changing technologies and circumstances. During their wars of conquest in the fifteenth century they were far ahead of the Europeans when it came to cannonry and naval mines; as a result, they were able to set up with amazing speed – for a people from the steppe – a redoubtable fleet.

Yet there was a downside: this innovative spirit would at times freeze into stubborn rigidity. The Ottomans were extremely fond of tradition and established custom, of ranks and classes, of calm and order. Even though military science in the rest of the world had developed by leaps and bounds, the eighteenth-century Ottomans, for example, used precisely the same tactics in their wars against the West as they had two centuries earlier.

In the nineteenth century, however, a new and ambitious phase began. The city's population of that day strongly resembled its counterpart in Vienna: variegated and lively, but also charged with tension. For an entire period in its history, in fact, Istanbul could not even be called a Muslim city: according to the Ottoman census of 1886 there were more Christians (444,294, to be exact) living in the entire Istanbul region than there were Muslims (384,386). But, just as in Vienna, more and more immigrants began pouring into the city; bitter and grudgeful, they soon upset the existing equilibrium.

More than a million Muslims from the Balkans and southern Russia, for example, had sought refuge within the Ottoman Empire after a series of massacres and plundering incursions – the memories of countless humiliations still fresh in their minds. A large proportion of them ended up in Istanbul. Tens of thousands of poor farmers, mostly Kurds, also came to the city around that time, often bringing with them a deep and lasting ill will towards the citified Christian Armenians. In addition one had the many thousands of Christian refugees driven in turn out of Anatolia by the Muslims. The famous *Handbook for Travellers in Turkey*, published in 1878, said, 'Eight or nine languages are spoken constantly in the streets, the shop windows bear five or six. The races have nothing that joins them; with the exception of commerce there are no relations between them; everyone lives in a state of permanent trepidation of the other.'

The empire was falling apart – or, more precisely, the decay that had been going on for centuries was now becoming apparent. There was more to blame than simply the smugness of the elite – although a more inquisitive, outward-looking brand of municipal leadership might have slowed the process. Istanbul, for example, had no open sea route to the rest of the world – Morocco blocked the only access between the Mediterranean and the Atlantic. The empire had been too slow and too late in following the technological advance of the nineteenth century. What's more, it had a new rival to the east: Russia, which was also modernising.

The Ottoman leaders reacted, as is often the case with decaying empires, with a reign of fear. They clung ever more grimly to the remnants of their crumbling world, saw enemies all around, thought themselves capable of resolving problems everywhere by violence and military interventions. Sultan Abdülhamid II (1876–1909), perpetually wary of assassination attempts on members of his household, locked himself away in his palace and ruled the country with an iron fist, abetted by an army of spies, censors and informants. All unfavourable news was excised by the sultan's censors, newspapers in Pera reported the assassination of the Shah of Persia as follows: 'His Majesty the Shah was not feeling well in the afternoon. His lifeless body was brought to Tehran.'

The revolution, when it came, started with a few hundred young Armenians. In reaction to the sultan's despotism, and inspired by the rise of Marxist and anarchist groups in Europe and Russia, they formed their own revolutionary nationalist movement. The first targets were 'treasonous' members of their own ethnic group: Armenians in the service of the sultan found their lives in danger. Then came the manifestos, demonstrations and armed confrontations, and the Ottoman pashas became worried: the Christians in Istanbul had not dared to oppose them openly since 1453. In the Turkish hinterland repression tightened: Kurdish militias were given free rein in beating down the real or imagined rebellion. Thousands of Armenians were murdered.

In 1895 some two thousand Armenian revolutionaries marched on the sultan's palace, armed with knives and pistols and shouting, 'Liberty or death!' They were counting on the support of the European powers, the establishment of a European peacekeeping force in the Armenian provinces and, if none of that came to pass, at least the support of Europe's working classes. But the government, as people said, 'released the rabble on them'. The bitterness of the Muslim population was skilfully exploited, thugs were allowed to beat Armenians to death with impunity, and hundreds of workers and recent immigrants, easily recognisable by their clothing, were killed. The slaughter went on for two days, and in some neighbourhoods for up to two weeks.

One year later events repeated themselves. This time the catalyst was a series of bombings by Armenian revolutionaries, plus the taking of a large group of hostages at the head offices of the Ottoman Bank in Galata. Louis Rambert, a bank employee, saw with his own eyes how a number of Armenian boatmen were clubbed to death while a large, obviously delighted crowd looked on from the bridge. 'All Armenian homes and small shops are being attacked,' he wrote in his diary. 'People go in and sack everything. It happens almost without a ripple. Every Armenian they see on the street is killed.'

One day later, apparently by official order, the clubs were dutifully turned in to the police. More than six thousand people had been killed. The city, which had always been a sanctuary for minorities and the persecuted, had become a hunting ground. For the first time in centuries, refugees fled the 'Passing Place of the Universe' and the 'Gate to Happiness'.

Meanwhile, however, Turkish society continued to modernise. As old, parochial Islambol fell apart, its citizens sensed the approaching demise and reacted like respectable passengers on a listing ocean liner: discreetly, but with determination, they hopped the railing and boarded the shiny modern dream that had drawn up alongside.

It was a truly spectacular cultural shift, an almost unprecedented volte-face in mentality. Among the pedestrians on the bridge – as photographs from those days bear witness – European dress became the rule, traditional clothing the exception. The turban made way for the obligatory fez, the men shaved off their beards, even Ottoman Turkish became less common. Arabic and Persian were no longer the second languages of choice. French was setting the tone.

The harem, still a normal phenomenon only a few decades earlier, came to be seen as a bizarre vestige of barbaric times: the 1907 census showed that only 2.16 per cent of the city's married men had more than one wife. When he returned to the city in 1903 Pierre Loti, who had courted disaster with his affair in 1877, received a hero's welcome. The German orientalist Max Müller, describing the hubbub on the bridge in 1897, was struck by the number of women in what he had expected to be an almost exclusively male crowd. 'The Eastern women, dressed in white, red, blue, green and purple garments, walk calmly and without fear across the bridge; their greatest beauty is their dark eyes, which shine from behind their transparent veils.' An increasing number of militant women actually began appearing in public without head-scarves. Indicative here is a cartoon from the magazine *Hayal*: two women meet on the street, one dressed traditionally, the other in modern apparel. First woman: 'Daughter, what kind of outfit is that? Aren't you ashamed?' The other: 'In this century of progress, *you* are the one who should be ashamed!'

Modernity, at least during that period, almost inevitably went hand in hand with the concept of the 'national': national pride, national progress. At first, as the British historian Phillip Mansel writes in his outstanding history of the city, the traditional cosmopolitanism of Istanbul stood in 'heroic contrast' to the 'strident nationalism which dominates the political, intellectual and emotional life of other European capitals'.

Yet it was not long before Istanbul's 'liberal' and 'modern' elite fell prey to such thinking. 'The social, economic and cultural bonds created by living in the same city', Mansel writes, 'could not outweigh the emotional satisfaction, the sense of righteousness, solidarity and self-sacrifice, provided by nationalism. The city was not enough: many inhabitants yearned for a state of their own.'

This sentiment was initially limited to the strongly European-orientated Armenians, but from 1889 it also grew among young, well-educated Turks. In accordance with the best revolutionary traditions, the Young Turks organised themselves in 'cells', secret clubs that had soon infiltrated seats of learning, the army and the public services all over the country. Before long, their leaders had to flee to Egypt.

When in July 1908 a mutiny broke out among the troops in Saloniki – many soldiers had received no pay for months – it spread across the empire so quickly that the sultanate was brought to its knees within a matter of weeks. Official censorship was abolished, amnesty was granted to political dissidents and a new constitution was drafted. That autumn free elections were held. This amounted to, quite unforeseen, the end of more than five centuries of Ottoman absolutism.

During this period Halide Edib recalled watching a wave of people moving across the bridge 'who emanated something special, who laughed and wept with such intense emotion that, for a moment, every human shortcoming and deformity was completely forgotten'. When the leaders of the Young Turks returned from exile, tens of thousands stood waiting to greet them along the quays and on the bridge. From that moment on, real power lay increasingly in their hands.

A counter-movement arose. A fundamentalist clergyman known as 'Ali the Blind' publicly cursed the modern constitution. He demanded the implementation of the shari'a, the body of sacred Islamic law: cafés, theatres and photography were to be banned, and an end would of course be put to the freedom of Muslim women to come and go as they pleased. A huge crowd of his followers marched on the palace. When the sultan actually appeared, Ali the Blind cried out: 'We want a shepherd! A flock cannot live without a shepherd!'

Ali the Blind was imprisoned, but his following – traditional Muslims, but also many civil servants, military officers and other officials who had led a comfortable life under the old regime – continued to grow. Counter-revolutionary rallies were held in the Hagia Sophia, cries were raised for the imposition of the shari'a: 'Onward! If we fall, we fall as martyrs, do not give in!'

On the bridge, in April 1909, the editor of an anti-revolutionary paper was murdered. Conservative soldiers mutinied, demanding that the Young Turk government ministers and officers be dismissed, that Islamic law be adopted and that Muslim women be kept off the streets. A Dutch journalist, Kees Valkenstein of the *Algemeen Handelsblad*, happened to be on the spot and witnessed the revolt. 'Mutiny? No one seems to know. Then a great commotion on the bridge. Gunfire. Suddenly you feel all strange inside. What are you doing so close to this? A crowd of furious – no, fearful – people comes running off the bridge. Everyone around you is panicking. They run off, and you run along with them. Away from that bridge.'

Ultimately, the attempt to stifle the revolution failed. The sultan was deposed in April 1909 and banished to Saloniki. His brother assumed the throne. The palace complex of Yildiz, the administrative centre, was dismantled. Along with the leaders of the mutiny the chief eunuch was hanged from the bridge, and the two hundred and thirteen women in the sultan's harem were released and repatriated to their families, who were 'blinded by the beautiful faces, the charming manners and the luxurious garments'. The Ottoman parliament started functioning as a normal democratic chamber of representatives.

The city's ten thousand stray dogs were rounded up and dumped on a desert island in the Sea of Marmara. At first, ships' passengers could see them standing along the shoreline, waiting hopefully. After that, for nights on end a hideous howling could be heard coming from the sea. The last survivors devoured each other. Istanbul could finally move on as a modern metropolis.

It was high time for a new bridge. For years the paranoid sultan had thwarted all such plans, fearing that rebels might open fire on his soldiers from the new shops to be built beneath the bridge. Only after the events of 1908 could work start on the project. The bridge was to be a paragon of modernity, everyone was in agreement about that, but what kind of modernity? Was it to be French modernity, should the bridge reflect the elegance of the Pont Alexandre III or some other such bridge spanning the Seine? Should it be the modernity of Britain, that cradle of democracy? Or was solid, reliable German modernity best?

The French design was soon scrapped for practical reasons – it did not allow for shops or coffeehouses. The negotiations that followed foreshadowed the political dealings of the new century and that applied to Britain's role in particular. The Ottoman Empire had long enjoyed British support, partly because it served to check

Russia's power and partly because it formed a safe route to the colony of India. As late as 1908 a cheering crowd had pulled the carriage of the British ambassador across the bridge and all the way up the hill to his residence. It seemed most likely, therefore, that a British building contractor would claim the spoils.

Behind the scenes, however, British diplomacy had performed an about-turn – a strategic switch that without a doubt contributed to the Ottoman demise. According to the British reassessment Russia was no longer an opponent but a potential ally against Germany. At the same time there was a growing fear in London that the Turkish revolution of 'Jews and Freemasons' might spread to Britain's colonial holdings in the Middle East. In their arrogance, successive British ambassadors in Istanbul skilfully succeeded in further ruining the bilateral ties with the new Ottoman democracy.

Only the Germans, then, were left. In 1910, the 'Vereinigte Maschiner Fabriken, Augsburg-Nürnberg' began its construction activities. On 14 April 1912 the new structure was dedicated with the ritual slaughter of two black sheep. The old bridge was towed a few kilometres upstream where, rusty and dilapidated, it was still used until a winter storm blew it to pieces.

In this traditionally chaotic city, the fourth bridge was an unparalleled phenomenon: a straight stretch of boulevard, a smooth surface without bumps or potholes and all of it brightly lit. 'Yes, this is a very different thing indeed from the picturesque Istanbul we love so well,' wrote Ahmet Ihsan in the *Istanbul Postasi* of 5 April, 1328 (1912 by the Western calendar).

An avenue both extremely broad and extremely smooth, with pedestrian walkways on both sides wider than the old streets of Istanbul, and with on both sides a beautiful railing in the European style and tall electric streetlights. In short, a European street in the true sense of the term. And that creates a feeling of inexpressible space. We walk along the smooth pavement that our feet are not used to at all. We feel happy. We smile.

In that same year Istanbul became a city at war. Four Balkan countries – Greece, Bulgaria, Serbia and Montenegro – had banded together and moved against 'the sick man of Europe', as the Ottoman Empire was often referred to. A Greek army had taken Macedonia without much of a fight, then the city of Saloniki. The Greeks immediately began a 'campaign of Hellenisation': after five centuries, mosques were converted back into churches, Saloniki was rechristened Thessalonica and some four hundred thousand Turks were driven out of the newly Greek territories.

70

Istanbul was flooded with refugees. The Hagia Sophia was turned into a hospital for cholera patients. Camels were seen in Pera's Grande Rue; the army had commandeered all horses. The Greeks in the city, who had comported themselves for centuries as upstanding Ottoman citizens, now strutted laughing through the streets of Pera every time a Turkish defeat was announced. Their patriarch openly proclaimed that the Ottoman Empire was 'foreign to my race, my faith and my nation'. Everyone waited with bated breath.

By November 1912 the Ottomans had lost their entire European territory, with the exception of a buffer of land around Istanbul. The czar of Bulgaria, dreaming of vengeance for the events of 1453 and of making Hagia Sophia a church once more, had his carriages of state and his imperial costumes made ready for a grand entry. But Russia, along with the other European powers, had no desire to see a new Byzantine regime on the Bosporus; the straits were far too important. In addition, if the Bulgarians entered the city the Ottoman government would almost certainly be prepared to 'release the rabble' once more, and this time against Christians in general.

For the last time the European superpowers of the day joined forces in a common campaign: with the approval of the Ottoman government, a total of fourteen British, French, German and Russian warships dropped anchor in the Bosporus. In and around Pera almost three thousand marines occupied strategic positions to protect the Greek and Armenian populations. Meanwhile, the Bulgarian attack on the city had bogged down. A truce was signed in early December. The Young Turks capitalised on the defeat by staging a coup. Bit by bit, the sultan was becoming nothing more than a puppet.

For the man in the street the serene Ottoman way of life seemed to return for a little while. In his childhood reminiscences Irfan Orga describes the almost enchanted atmosphere in their little neighbourhood behind the Blue Mosque, the sheltered gardens round the wooden houses, the cooing of the doves, the light and the sound of waves from the Sea of Marmara that could be heard through the open windows. As a five-year-old boy he spent the holidays at his aunt's and uncle's country house on the Bosporus. In the evening he and his uncle would go rowing across the silvery water while his mother and aunt sat in their brightly coloured silk bathrobes, drinking coffee under the magnolias. They swam in the sea. Tanned and on their way home aboard the ferry, they waved to his uncle and aunt and all the servants who had gathered in that happy garden, 'and none of us knew that we were saying farewell to a way of life that would disappear from the face of the earth for ever'.

Three months later he heard the town crier enter the street, with a man beside him pounding a big drum: 'All men born between 1880 and 1885 are to report to the recruitment centre . . .'

It was November 1914, and at the beginning of the Great War the pro-German regime of the Young Turks had no intention of remaining neutral any longer. 'War against Mother Russia!' moaned the powerless sultan. 'But her corpse alone is enough to crush us!' The mufti of Istanbul – like his Christian colleagues in Berlin, Paris and London – called for a holy war: 'Those who die will be granted the honour of martyrdom!' Some Armenians, openly supporting the other side, walked the streets beaming at the news of the first Russian victories.

But one month later there was almost no bread to be had in the city. That winter the bridge was quiet and deserted. Supplies of gas and drinking water became unreliable. The German Kaiser Wilhelm II arrived on a state visit; in the jerky newsreel footage you can see him riding across the bridge in full regalia, between long rows of marines and sailors.

In the spring of 1915 some two thousand four hundred prominent Armenians were transported out of Istanbul without warning. Nothing more was ever heard from them. Soon rumours began circulating about mass deportations and massacres of Armenians in Anatolia. At the start of the war the Young Turks had proposed to the Armenian nationalists an alliance: were they to start a revolt in the Russian region of Armenia, they would then be allowed to form an autonomous state under Turkish protection. The Armenians rejected the offer and opted for neutral status. But when the Turks suffered a major defeat in the Caucasus, blame was placed in part on the Armenian rebels, who were said to have started their own 'popular war' against the Ottoman Empire. After that the Young Turks considered them traitors who had to be 'neutralised' in order to quash their ambitions for an independent state.

During this period of uproar tens of thousands of Kurds and Turks were killed, but what happened to the Armenians in 1915 was of a different order of magnitude: a total of some seven to eight hundred thousand – some estimates say as many as 1.5 million – Armenian men, women and children 'disappeared'. They were marched en masse to Syria – still an Ottoman province at the time – and during the harsh desert crossing most of them died of exposure or disease, or were simply murdered. As early as 24 May 1915, the governments of England, France and Russia published a joint communiqué that spoke of massive killings of Armenians and the destruction of at least a hundred Armenian villages close to Van. Four months later, after a meeting with the cheerful Turkish Minister of the Interior on 30 September, 1915, the acting Austrian ambassador wrote, 'It seems that the plan to destroy the Armenian race has succeeded.'

Mustafa Kemal, however – better known by the name 'Atatürk', as founder of the Turkish nation – was furious about this 'shameful deed'. He would have liked to see those Young Turks responsible 'strung up' for their part in the killing and banishment of 'millions of our Christian subjects'. Istanbul's municipal statistics speak for themselves: the Armenian proportion of the population, 25 per cent in 1915, had fallen to 8.5 per cent by 1920. Two out of every three Armenians had 'disappeared'.

The first Allied bombs fell in October 1918. By 11 November even the proud Young Turks had to admit that the war had been lost. British warships anchored in the Bosporus and in the spring of 1920 Istanbul was occupied by Allied soldiers. The French General Franchet d'Esperey entered the city in triumph, astride a white charger, a present from the Greeks: a none too subtle reference to the white steed on which Mehmet II had made his entry in 1453. The city remained under foreign rule for almost five years, a period during which the Greeks and other minorities were increasingly perceived as collaborators. The clash between the nationalists and old, multicultural Istanbul was to become more bitter than ever.

★

The former Ottoman Empire was divided among the victors. The King of Greece was to be allowed to realise his dream of a new Byzantium, to seize and occupy mordant Istanbul and Anatolia, on condition that he also deal with that 'gang of robbers', the Young Turks. Under the leadership of Mustafa Kemal, however, and amid great bloodshed, a halt was put to the Greek invasion. On 29 October 1923 the Turkish Republic was proclaimed, its new capital Ankara. After more than fifteen hundred years, Istanbul had taken second place. 'Perhaps the waves of the entire Black Sea must roll into the Bosporus and engulf everything,' Mustafa Kemal said, in order to 'cleanse' the city of the 'filth', the 'duplicity', the 'lies' and 'amorality'. The name of the Grande Rue de Pera was immediately changed to Istiklal Caddesi, the Avenue of Independence.

From the top down the new regime organised a perfect revolution. In late 1925 the fez – 'this symbol of ignorance, carelessness, fanaticism and aversion to civilisation and progress' – and other items of traditional clothing were banned by law. In its stead, for example, men were to wear hats, 'the headwear worn by the entire civilised world'. This was the start of a drastic turnaround. A city chronicler had once bemoaned his fellow Turks as 'you unfortunates, who look to the West while your ship quietly sails East'. At least officially, a radical end had now been put to that ambivalence. During that same winter of 1925 the Muslim lunar calendar was replaced by the Gregorian. Rather than the age-old Ottoman legal system – which included the Islamic laws – the Swiss civil code was adopted. Polygamy was outlawed. Arabic script was banned: the Roman alphabet was now the standard. Instead of Friday, Sunday became the official day of rest. Women were given the vote and all Turks had to choose a surname: like Atatürk, Father of All Turks.

Turkey was also to become a 'pure' country. During the First World War, the Swiss anthropologist and ethnologist George Montandon had developed the theory of the 'homogenisation of national states': to prevent further international conflicts over minority groups, states were to be 'unmingled' by means of massive 'population transplants', and 'cleansed' of 'non-nationals'. Under pressure from the League of Nations, Greece and Turkey were among the first countries to apply this theory. In their peace treaty of 1923 they agreed to a mutual 'ethnic cleansing': approximately 1.3 million Greeks and a little fewer than half a million Turks switched countries. Only in Istanbul were the Greeks allowed, for the time being, to remain.

Yet the most drastic measure, perhaps, was the secularisation of the Turkish nation. In the eyes of

Atatürk and his followers a state could not be modern and religious at the same time. Koran schools were shut down, the Dervish orders and their monasteries were banned, the caliphate abolished.

And, just briefly, the bridge once again served as the backdrop to a historical vignette: shortly before his definitive dethronement the last sultan, the last caliph, the last heir to the Ottoman throne, was given a ticket by a British policeman for overtaking a car on the bridge on the wrong side. Framed, that traffic ticket still hangs somewhere in the Dolmabaçhe Palace, and rightly so. It, like nothing else, announced the absolute end of the empire. All that had made the city so special had come to naught: the trading culture, the sultanate, the role of the capital, the dynamics of the open, multicultural metropolis.

Meanwhile Irfan Orga, that happy boy of 1914, had lost his father, his uncle and his home within the space of a year. He ate grass to still his hunger.

IV

The porter had been driven mad by a woman. He was born in 1929 – would you believe it? – the oldest man on the bridge, and he'd seen it all. And now he had fallen under the spell and was lost.

'Come on, let him tell you about it himself,' the cigarette boys said, pointing to an alcove behind the bus station. The man was sitting on an orange crate, smoking a cigarette. His wares were lined up on a chunk of the old city wall: a drab grey pair of trousers, a white woman's sweater, a blue woollen vest, a worn-out anorak. Turnover: an average of eight million a day. He lived like an African mercenary, in boarding houses or out on the street, one hand always on the hilt of his knife, never knowing what disaster or good luck the day would bring his way. His leather cap was his proudest possession.

'Money isn't everything, ma'am, see it as a gift,' he'd told her only last spring when she passed him one cold evening. He had been selling umbrellas then, under the bridge, and business had been going so well that day that he had given her an umbrella, just like that, because she had pretty eyes and because it was raining so hard. 'What can I do to repay you?' she'd said. 'A little conversation,' he'd said. 'Nothing but a little conversation.' They had gone to one of the cafés beneath the bridge, just to warm up a bit. And then they went to a hotel. 'You can always love a woman, no matter how old you are.'

He'd had twenty-six billion in a savings account, for his old age. 'Of course, I wanted to see a bit of life.' For two whole months they had bathed in the luxury of hotels and restaurants, until almost everything he had scraped together was gone. 'She's moved to another city now. She was almost sixty, but she still had a beautiful young body, pretty eyes, there were always a dozen men swarming around her. You know what she said to me? "Who are you, anyway? You have no money, no house, you don't have anything!" And, to tell you the truth, she was right.'

The old man had been working on the bridge for more than half a century. 'My parents died when I was sixteen. No one in the village wanted to take care of me, in the army they taught me to read and write, and after that I ended up here.' He sold fish and home-made fruit juice, helped to fasten the moorings of incoming ships, manhandled cargo around the city for twenty-five years. 'I have no idea what tomorrow will bring. I have no experience of being ill, illnesses have always stayed away from me. I spent five years in prison, escaped three times. No, I'm not afraid of much. Why should I be?'

He's seventy-seven; had he been any younger, he said, he would have killed her.

Spring has come, but the atmosphere on the bridge is tetchy and it just keeps pouring. 'Put up your hood, my friend, or you'll catch your death of cold!' the insole vendor exhorts me, his own tattered camel-hair coat stiff with rain. Today he's selling adhesive bandages and red penlight batteries, but no one's interested in his wares. The soldiers on leave, the ones he's been dreaming of, never materialised. When the weather is fine they always need batteries – no one knows exactly why – but he can forget about that now. Lately he's been living on dry bread again; this week he couldn't even give his youngest son enough money for a soft drink, he had to borrow it from the bookseller.

The lottery girl is still brimming over with yesterday's news, about the first prize won with a ticket sold her by her colleague a few metres further along. A television crew had come and her colleague had received one billion by way of a bonus. But she is worried too. Although she never reads the paper, she's been hearing about political violence everywhere: Molotov cocktails tossed at a city bus, at least ten people killed; a bomb that went off at the headquarters of a political party; in the north of the country a woman had blown herself up in a mosque; two girls had tried to detonate a bomb somewhere along the Black Sea – the thing went off prematurely. In a Burger King in the city a girl had been taken hostage by two crazed policemen; on the quay beside the bridge there had been an attempted bombing.

It makes her tense. The most important event in her life was the bombing of a synagogue close to her home. A number of people had been killed then. She had heard a loud thud, covered her ears, closed her eyes 'and after that the whole world changed'. Enormous clouds of dust blew through the streets, her family was forced to leave the house immediately because it was about to collapse, her brother was deafened. They were able to salvage only a few things. 'We live in another part of town now, we don't feel safe in our old neighbourhood.'

Another special police team has been deployed around the bridge, there are plain-clothes officers everywhere, on the pavements and in the galleries. The cigarette boys are having a hard time, they can't shift a single pack. They all enjoy the 'protection' of two 'bosses' and some of them have been laid off – yes, even the lowliest positions on the bridge can be lost. 'Everything's shut down tight, we can't do a thing,' Önder complains. 'The only time we can sell anything at all is between six and eight in the morning when there are no police around. We're Kurds, of course, which automatically makes us terrorists.' As if that weren't bad enough, he has another problem: the police arrested him before he was able to hide his goods. Two hundred packs of cigarettes. Not only did he lose those, but now he has to pay a fine of ten million per pack. A total of two billion, or three months in jail.

His younger cousin comes over, he had something similar happen to him last year. Prison life was no joke. 'Everyone tries to push you around and mess with you. If you've got money, then you get respect. You're in there with the worst of the lot, men everyone's afraid of. So you have to stay friends with them, and the only way to do that is to have money. When some new kid comes in, with a baby face, oh, boy… And your family can't help you, the only thing that counts is money. If you don't have money you're in big trouble.'

Önder sighs, he's going to have to try to wheedle that two billion out of his Belgian uncle. He can't support his family any more either, they'll have to go back to the countryside. Önder, whom I've never seen in anything but an optimistic mood till now, is sombre. 'We're done for. We don't have diplomas, nothing. The police ask us: "What are you doing hanging around here? Why don't you go home and join up with the terrorists?" But there's no future for us there, either. Those political guys all have a good education, they can talk!'

The tea vendor suffers under the heavy police presence on the bridge as well. His little cart and teapots have been confiscated three times and, what's worse, on the last two occasions they were things he had borrowed. He's set up a temporary tea tent now, a hole in the wall of the old bazaar, hidden from view with a tarpaulin. 'Back home they're living on whatever people will lend them. My father called me yesterday: "Why didn't you pay the electricity? Next week they're going to come and cut it off and we'll all be sitting in the dark!"'

His only hope is the television programme *Beacons at Sea*. He says he met the presenter of this reality programme on the bridge and the man saw something in his predicament. Every week they help a poor family back on to its feet, so why shouldn't it be his family this time? 'All I need is fifty million for the electricity bill!' Under the leaky canvas, the tea drinkers talk about his chances. The audition is at the end of the week.

At the Galata Café the waiter is also worried about the situation at home. There isn't a customer in sight, so he starts to tell us in vivid detail about the changes that have turned life in his village upside down in recent years. Because if you think nothing ever happens out there in the middle of nowhere you can think again! The young people still don't have enough money for an Internet connection, but it's only a matter of time. The arrival of mobile phones alone created a minor revolution. 'All the shepherds have one these days. Until not so long ago they went off into the mountains for weeks with maybe a transistor radio for company. They often didn't even have bread with them and when they had to go into town they walked along the side of the road. They were all as poor as poor could be; they didn't even have soap. They had no idea what was going on in the world, not even in their own villages. But these days they call their wives three times a day.' The men know everything that goes on now and take part in every decision. The women have got the rough end of the deal.

We start talking about the women in his village. They still live very narrow lives, he says. Secret love affairs are a serious matter: a woman like that might even be stoned to death. Most of them can't read or write. When the Internet arrives it will pass most of them by and books don't mean anything to them at all. He doesn't expect that to change much, not in the near future. 'Their spirit is frozen,' he said. 'But on satellite TV they've started seeing things that would never, ever have occurred to them before!'

I ask whether he has changed himself, now that he lives on his own in the city. He feels more strongly now about traditions like stoning and

85

blood revenge, yes, he finds such excesses even more disgusting than before. And he also realises that because his wife is illiterate, his own children are receiving a limited education. That worries him more and more: how can they ever go to school like that, to get a twenty-first-century education? 'A woman can change, of course,' he says. 'Even this napkin can change. But if you don't send a woman to school, how can she ever know anything about modern life?'

I confront him with the attitudes I hear expressed by a lot of men around here: that's her destiny, she has to learn to live with it, alongside the husband her parents have chosen for her. 'Let's talk frankly, man to man,' the waiter says. 'Just imagine. You've got this newly married couple, they don't even like each other, but they have to stay together nevertheless. The coldness between them grows, the woman can't read, she can't find a job. All she can do is argue with her husband. And the children are stuck in the middle. If a woman like that could pack up and leave, if the couple could get a divorce, the children would probably have a much nicer childhood. Take it from me: in the end all these traditions only lead to more chaos.'

And so we chat away the wet, boring afternoons. I'm gradually starting to work out the pecking order on the bridge. First you have the hierarchy of the mobile phone: who can afford one and who can't? A mobile phone expands one's trading network enormously, and with it comes the possibility of getting lucky and perhaps, some day, hitting it big. Many of the cigarette boys have one, as does the pavement photographer, the lottery girl, the perfume vendor and the bookseller. The insole vendor and the old porter can only dream of phones.

Then there is the hierarchy of rich and poor, although on the bridge it is rather difficult to know exactly where that distinction lies: some of the bridge people, who I know are not too badly off, walk around in rags anyway, while others, despite their grinding poverty, always look fairly neat. The bookseller, for example, is in financial trouble all the time, but his teeth are in excellent condition. The woman who always sits on the steps leading to the tunnel, begging plaintively, wears too much jewellery and fine-looking shoes. No one really knows how the umbrella vendor is faring. He's away a lot these days, he has probably found a better spot in a nearby tunnel complex, but on the bridge people say he has a big secret: he's rich. He owns a house at the seaside, his wife has her own car, his children go to school. 'He's only here because he's bored, because he doesn't want to stay at home with his wife,' the gossips claim.

And then, of course, there is also the status derived from natural authority, with the pavement photographer – 'He's known us all since we were kids' – at the top of the heap and the junkies way down at the bottom. 'This can be a rough part of town at night,' the bookseller says. 'But I fear no one, except God.' The boys who have just come out of prison are the worst, they hang around him almost all evening. 'This week there was one of those kids, he'd read *Papillon* while he was in prison, he was determined to get that book from me. But he wouldn't pay for it. He threatened me, I finally had to beat him until he went away.' He shows me his secret weapon: a pair of flashy-looking knives attached to his key ring. 'My senses are keen.'

His friend the insole vendor was once caught in the middle of a shoot-out between gamblers. One of the men was killed on the spot, the insole vendor took a bullet in his thigh, 'a souvenir of the bridge', he calls it. He never has any problems with the junkies, though: 'I know those kids, and they know me. If you hit them, they hit back. If you leave them alone, they won't do a thing. Except for some of those little glue sniffers; their brains have become completely twisted.'

The cigarette boys do a fair amount of sniffing too, he adds, especially in winter, to keep out the cold. A few days ago one of them could barely walk and had to be taken home; he'd gone through five tubes in a row. Önder, who won't touch the stuff any more, has to admit: 'Glue makes you feel nice and warm, you forget the cold and the rain, you feel good.' He tells me about the fine points of sniffing – 'That yellow glue they use to fix shoes is the best, but it costs a million a tube' – and at the same time showers me with admonitions: 'Watch out! It's so incredibly addictive, you try it once and you're hooked.' I ask him about his own experiences. Laughing, he shows me a sizeable cut on his shoulder: only last week he was attacked by glue sniffers, but all he lost was a little blood. They weren't able to get to his money. 'Do you and your friends often have problems with criminals like that?' He laughs even louder: 'No, not really. *We're* usually the criminals.'

The older ones on the bridge are always talking about the future. They're all proud of the future, they all feel confident about the future, everything will turn out fine in the future. Not for them personally – most gave up on that idea long ago – but for their expanded, ramified, extended selves. Almost all of them have children somewhere, and almost all of those children have climbed further up the social ladder than they have. The umbrella salesman couldn't achieve his ideals through politics, but with his own private world he succeeded: all his children have had a good education. They same goes for the bookseller, the Spanish couple, even the insole vendor. Thanks to grants and state universities, those four alone have produced at least a dozen well-educated children – the same way underdogs all over the world are currently producing millions of excellently schooled young people.

In that respect the bridge is still very much a village, an unassailable system for survival with the family as its pivot point: the family, which provides protection against illness and other misfortunes, security in turbulent times, support in one's old age, safety in a nasty world.

What is the lottery girl working for? If you talk to her for a while, she'll tell you: 'To buy a house for my family.' Why does the insole vendor, despite his advanced age, still dream of emigrating? 'In order to give my sons a better future.'

A handful of recent titles from the series of popular novels are on sale at most kiosks: *Child Hero*, *Bomb*, *First Love*. So far, nothing unusual. But then: *When Leaves Turn to Yellow* – the cover shows a greying father, facing him a rebellious daughter without a headscarf – *Three Words of Advice* – a grandmother is breaking a loaf of bread that appears to contain a treasure – *A Family's Life Ruined* – here the cover shows a child leaving home, suitcase in hand.

'Tradition' and 'honour' are the central concepts binding this entire series. Turkish even has a special word for family honour, and such matters are instinctively given more weight than those of honour alone, particularly when the behaviour of women is concerned. Hence the critical appraisal of possible sons- and daughters-in-law, whom — because certainty is paramount — one finds preferably in one's own circles. Hence, too, a world-view that time and again grants higher priority to that which is 'characteristic of us' than to adapting to a new situation. To accept an interruption in the line of family relationships constitutes a foolish risk, an unnecessary undermining of the Permanent Life Insurance Policy.

One of the fishermen kept coming up and talking to me; he thought it was a nice project, this book. 'Everyone on the bridge has a secret, haven't they?' he said one afternoon. 'Well, so do I.' He confided that he was 'just like the perfume vendor in the gallery, the one with the toupee. You know what I mean.' Then he launched into a thousand and one stories. About men, the fathers of three or four children, who lived lives of never-ending duplicity. About men who bumped into their own sons at certain clubs. 'The city's full of bars and clubs, the potential is enormous, but everyone's scared. It's a weird world, full of secrets, embarrassment and desperation. The poor men. The poor women. Everyone is pretending.'

Within these families there is no room for

dissidents, for boys or girls who want to be different, who wear modern clothes, embrace the values of a new world and, at the same time and like all children, want nothing more than to be their parents' sons and daughters. In honour cultures you're either in or you're out; any middle road is less travelled and full of pain.

Almost every week the papers report cases of blood revenge, between thirty and fifty a year. 'Virgin suicides' are also becoming more common: to avoid confrontations with the police and the courts, girls are increasingly being pushed to commit suicide and so preserve the family honour. In one town in the south-east, Batman by name, no fewer than thirty-six women took their own lives during the first six months of 2006.

The people in the tea tent shook their heads in dismay; to most of them blood revenge was a sign of backwardness and failure, a scandal in its own right. Almost no one they knew would go that far, yet they all had their stories. About a country girl, for example, not so long ago, who was engaged to be married to a boy from the same village. But she went to the city, where she fell in love with another. Someone from the village saw her walking there, pulled out a pistol and killed her on the spot. That act of vengeance had nothing to do with morality, but with honour – a subtle, yet vital, difference. The extended family in this case included the whole village, and the father's and brothers' shame at being unable to keep the girl under control tainted the honour of the entire community; it constituted a life-threatening disease that simply had to be eradicated.

'There aren't many rules on the bridge,' the bookseller says, 'but there's one I always try to stick to, if only out of self-preservation: keep your hands to yourself – don't steal – watch your mouth; and keep your dick in your trousers.' Even the mild-mannered bookseller once spent a few weeks in jail in connection with a conflict of family honour – but he doesn't feel like discussing it.

The past, it's sometimes said, is a foreign country, a different continent. But this also works in reverse: a foreign country, that is our past. The springs and motives of our ancestors are things which most of us, as modern, secular Westerners, can but partly comprehend. Religious motivations, for example, often played a major – if not overruling – role in their lives, and to discover that we need go back only two or three generations. Entire family feuds were fought out over matters of honour – that too was not so very long ago, on that different continent that was Europe.

In this city, on this bridge, the concept of 'honour' is very much alive and kicking. As a guest in his country, the insole vendor will always offer me a cup of tea, even if that costs him half of what he's earned during a morning's shivering. Never will he accept a cent from me, not even if his stomach is groaning in hunger. When the perfume vendor tells everyone how wonderfully his son's career is coming along, he's probably not telling the truth, but no one would think of passing judgement: it's his way of boosting his own honour and status a little, and we all respect that. Although quite a few people on the bridge live on the brink of starvation, one sees remarkably little begging. One who begs, after all, has fallen to absolute rock bottom; for one who begs there is no going back, he has sold his self-respect and, along with it, his soul.

That same motif runs through the newspapers and public life. Honour, religion, politics and history all flow together almost unnoticed. Never doubt the glorious unity of the Turkish nation – not even if you know how forcibly that has sometimes been forged. 'Honour' comes to the rescue of one's own culture when it seems to shudder beneath the weight of the East–West dichotomy. 'Honour' keeps upright any wavering national self-image. Anyone daring to use the term 'genocide' in connection with the disappearance of hundreds of thousands of Armenians can easily find him- or herself in court. That is a matter of honour. Never talk about Kurds or Kurdistan, my companion Onur warns, but always of 'south-eastern Turkey'. A question of honour. In 2005 twenty-two Turkish publishers, forty-seven authors and forty-nine books were the subject of such legal actions, and even translators are fair game. Honour! And in that same year the Turkish prime minister filed fifty-nine complaints against authors and journalists for 'violating his rights and liberties' – in twenty-one of those cases, the writer was found guilty. Honour!

I enter into conversation with the blind flautist from the tunnel, who in fact only wears sunglasses for effect and after working hours can often be found quietly reading a newspaper. He used to be a policeman, but got into a violent argument with his boss after a soccer match with the young people of the village. That marked the end of his civil-service career. He hasn't seen or spoken to his children for twenty years. 'We divorced over ethical matters, let's leave it at that.' For all of those twenty years he has been living in hotels. He likes to imagine himself as the final defender of the Turkish flute, now that every shepherd on every mountainside has traded in his for a Walkman. 'I've got plenty of friends, look, here's my address book, it's packed.'

He is happy these days, he tells me; he's stopped drinking, has no regrets, all he wants is to live in peace. 'Sometimes I think: I should finish that woman off. But I'm fifty-six, I don't want to spend the rest of my life in jail.' Once he actually did shoot her; she was wounded, 'but unfortunately I failed to kill her'. He made an unsuccessful attempt on her life with a knife as well. Looking back over his days like this, he says, he sees that there are probably six or seven people he should have bumped off. 'They don't do that in Northern Europe, I know, not in France or America either. But around here there are things we refuse to forget.' He wasn't even invited to his daughters' weddings. 'They were scared that I would shoot their mother. And they were right. Because of that scandal, I might have ruined their marriages too. I didn't want to do that to them.'

Feelings such as hatred and fidelity also play a role, of course, yet – in much the same way that a merchant keeps his feelings out of his business dealings – they exist, as it were, outside the concept of 'honour' itself. Honour has value as a social currency, a dollar or a euro or a banknote of one million in the savings account of human happiness. Just as with real currencies, the value of honour depends on a host of factors, both tangible and intangible: factors such as wealth, education and prospects for the future, but also the respect and trust one has gained from others. In the course of the centuries the concept of honour has become entangled with all kinds of religious traditions, but it is not religious in origin: the 'cultures of honour' within the Turkish and Arabic worlds existed long before Mohammed and the Koran appeared on the scene.

Cultures of honour are, therefore, anything but exclusively Muslim: a phenomenon like blood revenge – some five thousand cases of which are reported each year worldwide – is seen regularly among non-Muslims as well, in countries as diverse as Turkey, Brazil, India, Ecuador, Pakistan, Egypt, Jordan, Morocco and Uganda. Medieval and Victorian chivalry in Western Europe, French and Polish patriotism, German military discipline, Dutch middle-class respectability, the imperturbability of the British upper class, but also the codes of behaviour of London street gangs all were – and to a certain extent still are – expressions, violent or otherwise, of a culture of honour. In something like the last seventy-five years, the concept of honour has largely disappeared from the Western body of rational thought. And although we are still familiar with the accompanying emotions – after 11 September 2001, for example, it was clear that America would have to strike back, where and at whom was not so much the issue – we are often no longer able to rationalise them. These days we think in terms of guilt and morality, with all the shades of nuance that go along with them. Honour, however, remains a matter of black or white, virgin or whore, insider or exile – a completely different world of thought from the subtle, analytical, eternally ambivalent considerations and compromises typical of the liberal West. Hence the difficulty we

Northern Europeans have in understanding societies in which honour and respect still count for a great deal.

While I was loitering around the tea tent and the Galata Café, a few streets away the Turkish action movie *The Valley of the Wolves* was playing in at least four cinemas. Along with *Bambi*, it was most popular film of the year and one of the greatest box-office successes in the history of Turkish film-making. In it a Turkish hero mounts a one-man offensive against the injustices and humiliations to which his Iraqi fellow believers are being subjected. All the gruesome incidents of recent months were re-enacted in detail, albeit with an extra dash of anti-Semitism; in all other ways it was simply a *Rambo* film turned upside down: the villains were the fresh-faced, blue-eyed Americans, the heroes this time the bearded militants and the girls in headscarves. When the worst of the villains was finally run through with a knife and expired with a long, echoing death rattle, the entire audience breathed a sigh of contentment. It was the same kind of audience that will no doubt embrace the real *Rambo* just as warmly next time. Yet what made the film unique in Turkey was something very different. The main father figure in the story is no longer a kind of Atatürk, a nationalistic hero, but a sheikh, a dignified spiritual teacher. The film's implicit message, therefore, is clear as can be: it is no longer the secular state that is the ideal instrument for protecting the world from chaos and injustice, but Islam.

It was during those same weeks that a mad controversy arose between East and West. In a reckless reaction to the fears of some illustrators, a Danish newspaper printed twelve cartoons depicting the Prophet Mohammed. Portraying the Prophet is in itself taboo in the Muslim world, and when this Jutlandesque incident became known in Pakistan, Indonesia, Malaysia and the Arabic countries a full-blown cartoon war broke out. Back before the Internet transformed the world into a village, such a pinprick – at least as seen through Western eyes – would have gone unnoticed; now, however, it led to a head-on collision between two very different worlds of thought. On one side you had the prophets of Western individualism who expounded the principle of absolute human freedom, including, in its most extreme form, the (putative) 'right to insult'. Raging on the other side were the fundamentalists of an agrarian tradition in which community, family and, above all, the concept of honour took pride of place. What followed were riots and demonstrations, mostly orchestrated by the relevant regimes – flags were burnt, cartoonists were forced into hiding, and all of it accompanied by a deafening row in the media and, out in the streets, more than a hundred people killed and eight hundred injured.

On the bridge, everyone is far too busy making ends meet to pay much attention to the news – Önder was the only one who knew anything about the religious murder of the Dutch film maker Theo van Gogh – but the cartoon conflict made tempers flare in the tunnels and beneath the dripping eaves. 'Idiots, maniacs, those cartoonists,' Önder railed. 'They have no right, this is our faith, and they have to respect that.' 'All wars begin with provocations like this,' the waiter growled. 'We see everything on TV, we hear and know everything,' the insole vendor said. 'And we are very angry. I'm a human being, you're a human being. God gave us the Koran and the Bible, and we have to respect each other like that. If something like this happened to the Christians the whole world would be up in arms!'

Gradually I came to realise that the cartoon question, at least on the bridge, might mean something very different from what I had first suspected. During those weeks I never heard a bad word about Christians or other non-Muslims. Perhaps people were only being courteous, but I tend to think not. This, after all, was not about hurt religious feelings as we know them. It was, above all, about wounded pride. And when you are as poor as a church mouse, honour is one of the last assets you have left. None of those people I spoke to regularly were fundamentalists, with the possible exception of Önder, but he was a man of the world too. He was also the only one who felt that Theo van Gogh had been killed justifiably: 'Too bad for him, but he deserved to die. He insulted Islam.' When I told the other people in the tea tent about Van Gogh's murder, they reacted in shock. 'Only God can see to it that a person is born,' the insole vendor said. 'Only God may take a life away.' He and his friend the bookseller, in fact, detested all those hirsute hypocrites who sat around all day fulminating in the teahouses, yet never lent a helping hand to an impoverished fellow human being.

'I attend to my duties, no one can deny that,' the insole vendor declared. 'I never attend mosque any more, but I go there to feed the pigeons.' The only reason the waiter considered himself a Muslim was because that was how he was raised. 'I believe that there's one God and that all religions present a different version of him. And then they wrote holy books about him to serve their own purposes.' When I asked whether he observed the obligatory periods of fasting, the tea seller burst out laughing: 'For me, every day is Ramadan!' But, without exception, they were all religious in some sense and felt sincerely offended by this cartoon business.

Interesting to note was the selective nature of their outrage: when a Sunni suicide bomber blew up a Shi'ite mosque in Iraq on the first day of Ramadan no one mentioned it. They talked about a handful of cartoons, but not about twenty-five fellow Muslims murdered in their own house of prayer on the holiest day of the year. They were scandalised by the West, but not by the East. Religion, for my acquaintances on the bridge, was not merely a source of comfort or forgiveness, but above all a feeling that binds them in their complicated relationship with the affluent West.

'My village is full of people who don't know a thing about the Koran. But at the same time they're prepared to die for Islam,' the waiter tells me. Without religion he himself would lose contact with the ground beneath his feet; he would, as it were, disintegrate, and that goes for the insole vendor and the bookseller as well – at least, the way the situation is now. Not because they are particularly devout – all three call themselves 'humanists' or 'scientifically religious' – but because religion, in the waiter's words, 'lies close to our soul and spills over into it'. Anyone who mocks their god, therefore, is not insulting an institution or even a religious feeling; no, he is dealing a blow to their deepest sense of personal worth, the last bastion against total humiliation.

For a few hours each Friday, Önder would abandon his little club of cigarette pedlars. He would go to the nearby mosque to pray and just to sit. He had once ended up there more or less by accident and the serenity of the place exercised an enormous attraction on him: 'When I pray I feel so relaxed. Suddenly all the stress is gone. Suddenly there's peace.' On one occasion he allowed me to go with him. I would be better off as a Muslim too, he thought. 'It's the best religion there is, plus you get to go to paradise!'

We washed at the fountain in the courtyard and in a whisper he regaled me with the Minor Catechism according to Önder. 'It really helps. When I come here and I pray, it helps me with my problems.'

Does praying also help you to get into paradise? 'Of course. I don't know what will happen to me in the end, but at least I do my duties.'

So what was paradise like? 'It's more beautiful than anything you've ever seen in the world; you've never seen anything like it.'

Who gets to go there? 'You Christians don't go to paradise. And if you're a Muslim and you haven't done your duties, you go to hell too, but only temporarily.' Did that mean you should fight against the unbelievers, the way some people claimed? 'There will be a struggle, but without physical violence. It's about belief, about thoughts. You have to respect them. Every person sins in his own way and does good in his own way. Only, if that respect is no longer there, well, then . . .'

The muezzin started again, his sing-song cry sounding tinnily from the minaret's loudspeakers: 'Allahu akhbar . . .' When I asked Önder to translate what he was saying, he shook his head. He'd never understood it either. 'It's all Arabic, no one here knows what it means. We pray in a foreign language.'

I was reminded of what V. S. Naipaul once wrote after a journey through four non-Arabic Muslim countries: 'Everyone not an Arab who is a Muslim is a convert.' To a certain extent the same applies to modern-day Turkey. According to Naipaul, the convert's world-view alters. His religion, after all, is an Arabic one, his holy places are in Arab lands, he must forget his own history and become a part of the Arab story, whether he likes it or not. 'The convert has to turn away from everything that is his,' Naipaul wrote. 'The disturbance for societies is immense, and even after a thousand years can remain unresolved.' The enormous tiled dome, taut with its countless motifs, stretched out above us.

The Bridge

Said Faik (Abasıyanık)

If no one crosses the bridge,
Does the bridge think

Of the idiot passing by, waving clothes pegs
In ecstasy before his eyes?
Of those who sit sunbathing
Along the dock at Üsküdar?

Of what lies beyond the shore at Üsküdar,
Kastamonu, Sivas, Safranbolu . . . Erzurum?

Among the people here, binoculars
Have blossomed like roses.
Here dough-makers roll – from inner dough –
Transparent, web-fragile dreams of home,
    with gigantic rolling pins.

Pale, fat sweet-sellers with blushing cheeks,
Blithe as they slap down sourballs and toffees
on the marble counter,
Here fall out of character, wax poetic
Their hands redolent of sesame nougat
That crackles as it's cut with giant knives
Handsome, big people
Like the waxen busts of janissaries in the military
    museum
They stand here shoulder to shoulder

With good people grown fat from their pastries
    made with bad butter,
And peer down at the diver.

People standing with little fingers interlocked.
People in their yellow garb.
Having lived through hot nights in the village without geese
The cracking frost and the earthquakes, the floods and wars;
People who lived on skimmed buttermilk with foam,
    on boiled grain with the chaff still in it;

With little fingers interlocked . . .
Sometimes swooning in a sudden fit of epilepsy . . .
Where do they come from, where are they going?
With their pinkies intertwined . . .
They are the sleepwalkers of the bridge

At the age of twenty, thirty, they all dreamed the dreams
    of the greybeard;
Happy they are, happier even than the anglers themselves,
    when a mackerel is hooked
Below, in the boats where Istanbul's ruffians crowd
    together;
They love stale sesame buns, on sale, thirty paras apiece
It is all fast asleep in their hearts
Valour, friendship, affection and tolerance . . .
All necessities and the needed.

That man there, his neck shaven clean with a wicked
    razor
Hair slicked back,
Loose clothes, a golden glance, blond, long-legged,
Do you know who that is?

Not only the bridge knows him, but the old policemen
     too:
     – Oh no, you here again? they say.
He winces, takes his hands out his pockets, tosses
His cigarette butt on the ground
     – I was just leaving, gentlemen, fellows, he says.
It is the famous pickpocket, Istavro of Yedikule
And a fine young man by the look of him.

Another stands, past ten at night, looking at the boats and
     lights, and laughs.

Oh, if someone bought him a ticket it would be so easy
To travel the wide world round;
The man beside him thinks of staying, though leaving is
     what he wants
Except that with the latter all is fake, daydream and
     melancholy.
But those who wander round in search of a friend,
Keep them at arm's length.
On the bridge you don't make friends,
from the bridge you watch and see.

V

The Storm of the Windmills

Istanbul is a classic city, the way Amsterdam still was until halfway through the twentieth century: poverty has pitched its tent in the heart of the old city, the middle classes, ring after ring, live further and further away from that, while wealth – and that is abundant here as well, make no mistake – lives amid the greenery or in the chic neighbourhoods across the Bosporus.

In that way the city adheres to an ancient pattern. Even from the earliest days the hilltops of old Constantinople were reserved for the rich. From their homes and palaces the piss and filth trickled down incessantly – the city had no sewers – until it reached the sea. Social categories were determined by the same movement, but from bottom to top: the lower a house stood on the hillside the more rubbish and filth collected around it, and the more humble its inhabitants' status. Those who lived at the foot of the hills therefore lived amid the shit of the wealthy to boot; there was nothing to be done about that. Those were the neighbourhoods where the insole vendor, the old porter and the blind flautist had their lodgings, and most of the cigarette boys too.

On one of those downward currents, past the streets with their tinsmiths, pump mechanics and electricians, lived the bookseller. You had to climb three sets of concrete stairs and push aside a worn-out door before finding yourself in a workroom packed with merchandise and cherished souvenirs: old toy cars, pen sets, bottles, model train carriages, a handful of CDs, a light-blue plastic toy caravan, a calendar from 1994, a book of poems by Nâzim Hikmet, the red mudguard of a child's bicycle. He lived alone. Ten years ago his wife and their ten-year-old son were killed in a road accident. He still had a daughter, but she went to school in another city. The products with the highest profit margins are the remainders he buys at state auctions. Twelve thousand of those child's bicycle mudguards are tucked away in a warehouse. That transparent plastic belt with the little bear on it: he has twenty thousand of those for sale. Old photographs go well, too. There is one man on the bridge who will buy any photograph featuring a child with a toy. A good customer.

The bookseller has thin features, a wispy moustache, lively eyes. 'I don't do a lot of talking,' he says. 'I don't try to compete with the others.

When they go home I open my bookstand, every day, from six thirty to nine. I don't sell any old books; I specialise in photography and poetry. My customers are very particular and they know how to find me, they're students, even a professor. Look, here's a book about Holland, for example.' He shows me a spotted and stained guidebook from the 1980s. His private library occupies three shelves. Turkish titles, but also Pablo Neruda, Alexander Pushkin, Mayakovsky, Knut Hamsun, he lets the names roll over his tongue. 'They taught me everything, what people are like, how to deal with them.'

When the driver who killed his wife and son was sentenced to only twenty days in jail, he was so furious that he refused to pay taxes any more, with all the consequences that brought. 'I'd never had anything to do with the police or the courts. But when they died because of him and he was barely punished, I didn't want to have anything more to do with the law.' In the end, his brother paid his debts and bailed him out of prison. 'I went completely mad after my wife's death, I spent three years just wandering the streets.'

He never remarried, he didn't want to burden his daughter with a stepmother. 'My wife died, she was everything to me, she was a part of my own body. My daughter and I, that's all my life consists of these days, so let it stay that way.'

★

It was the bookseller who introduced me to the
urban chroniclers. In my own city, Amsterdam,
there has always been a tradition of writers and
journalists who observe the rhythm of the city, year
after year, who pass on the major and minor stories,
who document the most trifling shifts in idiom and
behaviour, who test the mood of the market place,
can find their way blindfolded through the
corridors of the city hall, who know every criminal,
fool and drunkard, who have eyes, ears and noses
everywhere.

Here, it turned out, you also had chroniclers,
men of exactly the same ilk. A columnist like
Ahmed Rasim, for example, wrote his 'Letters from
Town' on an almost daily basis, including observa-
tions, complaints and commendations, always
spiced up with a little skilfully applied vitriol. This
semi-journalistic, semi-literary genre had originated
in Paris, and both my Amsterdamers and Rasim
clearly bore the mark of rebellious French street
writers like Emile Zola and Victor Hugo. In
Istanbul, however, Rasim had created a tradition of
his own, as spiritual father of a dynasty of urban
reporters that ultimately produced international
talents such as Elif Shafak and Orhan Pamuk.

Almost all of them have written about the bridge
at one point or another. In the 1930s, for example,
you had Nâzim Hikmet, who penned diatribes

III

about how long one had to wait at the open bridge: 'I reached the bridge at 6.20 . . . It was drizzly, the sky a solid grey, it was still almost dark . . . A crowd of people, men, women and children, stood waiting for the bridge to open on the Karaköy side. Another, identical crowd was waiting on the Eminönü side . . . If Istanbul is to start work at seven, the bridge cannot remain open until six thirty, let alone until seven o'clock next week!'

In 1944 Oktay Akbal described rush hour on the bridge: 'Each pavement has its own pedestrians: the sailors almost always choose the left, while the merchants and petty civil servants walk on the right. The factory girls are particularly fickle; they never seem to decide at all and walk one day down the right side, the next day down the left.'

These writers reported the huge ship's fires on the Bosporus in the 1950s and 1960s, describing oil tankers that exploded after a collision and set the whole sea on fire – once, as the journalists stood watching breathlessly on the bridge, one of those tankers had veered and come almost straight at them.

Rifat Ilgaz wrote verse about a pedlar's exhausting struggle to earn his daily bread: 'What must he eat then, stones? You can't do that to him, can you, Galata Bridge?'

In 1952 Yasar Kemal described a spectacular influx of bluefish around the bridge; the fishing boats were packed in so tightly that you could step from one to the next, there was no need for a bridge. For a whole week, life was a feast for the city's poor: 'Long live the bluefish! Thanks to you there is joy in every home! Long live the bluefish! May you be rewarded, bluefish! What a brilliant idea it was to come and visit us like this!'

And then you had Reşat Ekrem Koçu and his *Istanbul Encylopaedia*, a gigantic loose-leaf project that was published in instalments between 1958 and 1973. These days the huge binders have a cult status, they're almost impossible to find, and only after a great deal of difficulty were Onur and I able to get a look at one. Opening the binder, we found ourselves in a curiosity shop of the printed word, a fascinating collection of jokes, little-known facts, tall tales and runaway hobby-horses that went on and on for thousands of pages. The entries described districts, neighbourhoods, houses, fishing boats, handcarts, cafés, shops, warehouses and brothels. Koçu and his assistants met almost every day in a local tavern, and that men's-club atmosphere permeates the encyclopaedia they made. On page 5,894, for example, we came across a detailed description of one of Galata's leading whorehouses: '. . . and beside me then, right next to my ear, there was a snoring sound . . . I turned my head a little to look . . . what a gob! All the lipstick had peeled off it and the skin beneath looked purple and bruised .

. . and then that hair! And those teeth in that baggy mouth… canary yellow, and caked with algae along the gums . . .' The gentlemen also wrote eagerly about a host of murder cases, about 'bachelor quarters' frequented by 'bad boys' and 'handsome wine pourers', and an entire article was even dedicated to a 'skilled child acrobat between the ages of fourteen and fifteen' whom Koçu had 'encountered between 1955 and 1956'.

He and his friends were not around to see the demolition of the fourth bridge in the 1990s. To their great sorrow, undoubtedly, their life's work never got past the letter 'g', and because the Turkish word for bridge starts with 'k' we shall never know what this illustrious company had to say about our bridge.

It was a new generation of urban writers who huddled together as the present modern bridge arose beside the old one, which 'with her eight-thousand-ton body had borne the burdens and miseries of Istanbul for eighty years'. Can Yücel wrote of 'the entire zoological garden of history' that had crossed the bridge.

The city reporter for *Cumhuriyet* saw that the fishermen, who had eaten raw mackerel and drunk 'Nutuk' wine there the night before, had now disappeared. 'The smell of fish and wine still lingers in the silence of the morning sun that shines along the bridge's galleries.' He interviewed the last of the regular backgammon players in the coffeehouse, Master Ali, Uncle Hüseyin and Grandpa Mehmet. 'Look, here we are, all of us, in the picture. Everything's in it, in that picture, the worn pieces, the yellowed dice, the chairs that smell of autumn, the tables that smell of winter, the hookahs as old as we are . . . ' The bridge, he wrote, was a ship taking on more water all the time, soon to be swallowed by the waves. 'Behind it stands the new bridge, its gigantic muzzle open wide, ready to snap shut.'

Of today's denizens of the bridge only the old porter and the pavement photographer knew the old one, they were working here when the others were still in their cradles. The porter has never really grown accustomed to the new bridge: 'The old bridge was my life, nothing could compare to it. Back in those days I could afford a big bottle of raki every day, there was plenty of fish and the sun was always shining. What do we have like that today?' When talk turns to the old bridge, the photographer grows wistful as well. 'Everything happened there, everything was on sale there, it was truly fantastic. When that bridge was built we had a million inhabitants, by the time I started working as a photographer it was four million, now we have more than ten. We've become a huge city. It's all over!'

And now the season has come for the Storms of the Windmills, of the Black and the Red Plums, and for the Meltemi, the cheerful summer wind that whisks away all nasty fumes and feelings. The sun beats down on the pavement, the asphalt becomes softer and slower, dust settles over the city. The swallows have chased away the gulls and go screeching through the air everywhere: between the minarets of the big mosque, between the trams and taxis, between the lamp-posts above the bridge. A condom seller has appeared over by the control booths; he has rousing pictures of women in floral bathing suits. The contemplative fishermen of winter and spring have disappeared. At least three hundred rowdier fishermen have taken their place; they're pulling in sardines, filling big canning jars with half-dead fish. Every metre of railing is occupied, you hear shouting everywhere, there is even a little estate-agency trade going on in fishing spots, arguments break out each time lines or poles become crossed.

This is no place for a professional fisherman. 'The rods they're using are much too short, they just try anything, what a bunch of amateurs,' the old Spanish angler grumbles. He started work at five this morning and in the meantime he has seen the strangest things: a young man and woman who had slept in front of their poles all night; a rich couple who had offered him thirty million to fish all day for them, with their equipment, so they could show off the catch at home; a seventeen-year-old girl who

116

claimed to be homeless – an impossibility, according to our old friend, because this was one girl who would never lack a bed to sleep in.

The photographer is in high spirits. He has finally made his big investment: the old Polaroid has made way for an excellent digital camera with a pocket-sized printer attached. Proudly, he demonstrates this new wonder: the photograph slides back and forth three times through the buzzing little machine, first yellow, then red, then blue, and there we are! Yesterday he had eleven customers – forty-four million – because he can raise his rates now as well.

Things are going pretty well for the insole vendor, too. He's found a new job in one of the side tunnels, as custodian of the ladies' loos. The gents' has its own attendant, with his own cash register, but men aren't allowed in the ladies'. The only one in charge there is our friend, who sits on his stool outside the door all day, waiting for the women to drop him a few million. His leg still hurts, but now he's started saving for a visit to the doctor. His clothes look neater, he has a bit more contact with his children at the moment and that all comes as quite a relief to him. The only problem is that his new job isn't exactly what he'd hoped for. But maybe he can get on the payroll, as a cleaner for example, and then move up to running the cash register at the gents'. But a lightning career move like that will take some planning. And besides, he's starting to miss his freedom.

The old porter looks sombre, standing there beside his pile of worn-out trousers and vests. Has he had any business? 'Nothing, nada. Absolutely nothing. I'm an old man.' He starts on again about his big misstep, why on earth did he ever do that? 'Infatuation makes a man lose his mind, that's all it was. Your brains just go out of the window.'

The cigarette boys are back in the tunnel again, jabbering and joking away, but Önder doesn't seem at all happy. He's never going to be able to pay his fine, the police are still hassling him and he's only able to sell a few packs here and there. This time his family is actually going back to the village, they're leaving at the end of the week. He himself wants to go to Izmir: 'There are lots of tourists there, I'm sure I could find work in a café or restaurant.' The tea vendor and the perfume man are gone too. The tea vendor has closed up shop, it seems he's found a job at a petrol station. The perfume man has simply vanished into thin air, he is nowhere to be found. But the blind flautist plays away cheerfully. He has a new girlfriend, a Japanese woman. 'She's not much to look at, but we're good together.'

What do the men on the bridge talk about when business is slow, when they stop for a break on one of those pleasant, breezy days when the passing girls all seem to smile encouragingly? They talk about what's in the papers, chatter about the city. They talk about the old Istanbul stock exchange, just next to the bridge, which a pair of Kurds are planning to turn into a luxury hotel. They talk about the girth of the fish that was pulled in over the railing that morning. About a tourist with a pair of indecently short shorts. They make plans for an excursion to the little harbour at Ortaköy, to chase the girls. They laugh about one of their friends who speaks a little English and always meets foreign girls, but never gets them into bed because of his acne. They talk about 'open' and 'closed' girls, about girls without headscarves and girls with: in practice though, they assure me, it doesn't make any difference. They boast to each other about the closed girls they've known. Hard to seduce? 'No way! They're the easiest! You've got some girls who walk around completely wrapped up in sheets, but they'll do anything.'

It hadn't taken long for me to notice that 'open' and 'closed' are relative notions around here. You can dress more or less religiously and still, as they say here, have 'an open spirit' – or vice versa. I saw heavily veiled girls – or, more accurately, heavily veiled shapes – walking across the bridge, laughing and giggling with girlfriends in short skirts and vest tops. I saw a headscarf girl in a tight embrace with a boy with rings through his nostrils and tattoos on his arms. I saw Muslim punks and 'Islam fashionistas' in colourful, tightly tailored outfits with skirts split up to the thigh, refined make-up, bright headscarves. 'It is true that they wear veils in Pera,' the enterprising ambassador's wife Lady Mary Wortley Montagu wrote to a woman friend in 1718, 'but they are such that they allow a woman's beauty to shine through even better.' That, to a certain extent, is still the case.

According to the contemporary codes of the bridge, the headscarf has all kinds of connotations: religiosity, practical protection, chastity, subtlety, the past, the future. The shawl is the great compromise that can be adapted to meet all contingencies: worn secularly round the neck or gracefully covering the hair, whichever is religiously and politically most correct. 'The shawl allows you to negotiate all occasions,' say the women whom I ask about it.

The business community – with the exception of the religious sector – does not favour headscarves. Among civil servants tolerance varies, depending upon the tenor of the regime in power. After each major change of government women become either more 'open' or more 'closed'. The wife of a central bank official recently set the mood: she had always been 'open', but since the moderate Muslims have come to power she is 'closed'. You see the same pattern on the streets: the women of this city were always fairly open, now they're withdrawing increasingly behind the veil. It's still true that more 'open' women cross the bridge than 'closed' ones, but they are also harassed more. As their surroundings become increasingly 'closed', they make an easier target for the insults and the pawing of extremists and idiots.

One afternoon Onur and I come across a somewhat older woman amid the fishing public, a retired head nurse who moved to Istanbul long ago for family reasons. She sometimes does a little fishing herself, along with a former policeman she had befriended, but today all she's done is walk around and stare angrily out to sea. Why? 'Because of my daughter, sir. Thank God I was able to give her a good education. But then this Canadian came to Turkey, a businessman, they met and she went back with him. She's been living over there for the last four years, they have a child, my grandchild, but I've never seen him.' Her daughter called two days ago, she'd had an accident, she was terribly upset. 'And now I want to go there. But I'm a Muslim, so they won't give me a visa! I gave those Canadians a lovely, intelligent, well-raised daughter. She has a job, she's dependent on nobody, she's beautiful . . . what a stroke of luck for that country! So why are they doing this to me?'

She told us that she was the second of three

sisters, she had worked in any number of village clinics and now lived alone. Her ex-husband's conservatism had driven her out of the house. He had made a huge fuss about his Canadian son-in-law: 'I could even stand it if he was a criminal, as long as he's Turkish!' he'd shouted. She was from the European side of Istanbul, her husband from Anatolia. With the sure hand of an experienced teacher she draws us a little map. 'That's where Turkey turns rough, it's a different place altogether. Over here you still have lots of old immigrant families from the Balkans, the men are more modern, the women freer. And thank God, I received a good education. "I can do whatever I like," I told him, "and you can't stop me." So we got a divorce.'

Her older sister, she says, married exactly the same kind of man. But she's more timid. He cheats on her. 'Despite their fine ideals, our parents weren't able to protect us from men like that.' Their mother died when the sisters were in their late teens; that, she feels, is why everything went wrong. 'We, the sisters, suddenly had to make all our own decisions. Back then the tradition was to get to know your fiancé gradually, but we didn't have time for that. We met them, married and that was it.'

A few days later we meet her again, this time in the company of her older sister, a woman of about fifty who bears a striking resemblance to the actress Meryl Streep. The sister isn't allowed to leave the house without her husband's permission, our conversation is a serious transgression; for a while she even concealed from him the fact that she had a job. 'I'll tell him: "I went into town with my sister, we did some shopping." To tell you the truth, I'm not particularly courageous.'

Once they were married he pressured her into giving up her job. 'I was pregnant, I knew it wasn't going to be easy to live with that man, but my child needed a father. And now I have four daughters. Why? I don't know, that's just the way it went.' She speaks of thirty years of drunkenness and aggression. 'My daughters and I have created our own world, my girls lived beneath my wings. And thank God, the same thing won't happen to them, they're free now!'

'The world we're from was so different from that of those barbarians,' the head nurse says. 'Our mother was a democrat, our father a socialist. I can remember my mother travelling for hours to attend speeches by the leaders of her party. My father never tried to keep her from doing what she wanted. Not like our husbands: "My politics are your politics." Remember all the commotion when my daughter wanted to marry that Canadian?'

The older sister: 'I insisted on going to the wedding. My husband screamed: "If you go, our marriage is finished! With a foreigner! What a disgrace!" But Allah is great, he sees everything. All our daughters are either married or engaged to foreigners. One of them goes out with a German fellow, the other one has a Dutch mother-in-law and my oldest daughter is going to marry a Danish man.'

The nurse: 'OK, we're socialists, the men we married are nationalists; still, there's no reason why that has to be a problem. Seen from the outside, their social lives seem modern. But at home they expect total submission from their wives. A political difference of opinion is impossible, criticism is unthinkable.'

The older sister: ' "I'm the king around here," that's what my husband always shouts. If our husbands had been conservatives we'd be wearing headscarves now. These days, though, parties switch every once in a while and all you can do is go along with it, even in the way you dress!'

The nurse: 'When you started working again, in secret, you used to tell him you were visiting me. Remember that time he tried to call me, drunk as usual, to check up on you?'

The older sister: 'Thank God the line was out of order.' And then, a little later: 'You know, it's all to do with mothers. Our husbands were raised by their mothers, and according to their mothers' rules we, the women, had to obey unconditionally. I raised my daughters the way my parents did, as humanists who respect others. We lived like caged birds, but I wanted to give them an education and have them see the world. And that's what they did. They've flown, and soon this little bird will be flying too.'

The head nurse: 'That's a great idea. You're too good for him, you protect him all the time. When I come to visit I'm the one who argues with your husband, instead of you.'

We talk about religion, about the position of women in Islam, about how their religious beliefs can coincide with their struggle for emancipation. 'Of course, within Islam, men are dominant,' the nurse says. 'But total obedience and submission, that has nothing to do with it. When the Koran forbids women to do something, it forbids men to do the same.'

The older sister: 'I love my religion, I pray every night for my daughters and for my own salvation, I never fall asleep without praying.' They talk about the Prophet's own wife, a born businesswoman and as free as a bird. The rule that a man is allowed to take four wives, they say, began as an emergency measure: with so many wars being fought at that time there was a huge shortage of men. No, their faith sustains them. 'The time my husband tried to call me at my sister's house and I was saved by the phone being out of order, that was a sign, a helping hand from Allah!'

★

In 1749 the young Irish Lord Charlemont reported
that women in the harems reacted indignantly
when a Western female visitor told them about the
liberties enjoyed by women elsewhere. It was as
though they were hearing stories about the
nakedness of Indians, or free love in Tahiti. 'They
seemed rather to look upon such customs with
disgust and horror than with any degree of envious
desire.' Two hundred and fifty years later that
disgust with the West still echoes on for many
women in the Muslim world: pornographic,
decadent, morally corrupt, a dishonourable freedom
that humiliated women.

That summer of 2006 had seen the publication of
an extensive international survey – the Gallup
World Poll, based on eight thousand interviews in
eight Muslim countries – which showed that male–
female relations, at least in a domestic setting, were
not the top priority for most Muslim women.
Other issues were, in their view, much more
urgent. The women were particularly keen on
having the right to vote freely, to occupy senior
jobs and, above all, to work outside the home. The
most serious problems within their own world they
listed as the lack of unity between the Muslim
countries, corruption and violent extremism.

The most striking feature of the survey's results
was the outspoken support expressed by the vast

majority of women for the 'moral and spiritual values' of their own societies. And, at least as interesting, nowhere in the Gallup poll did the Muslim women themselves mention the veil and the burka – generally regarded in the West to be symbols of repression – as problems.

The head nurse – I spoke with her a great deal during those final weeks – had said much the same thing: 'In practical terms, economic independence is the most important factor for us. And getting a good education is a part of that. You can go on and on trying to make women aware of their situation – most women, by the way, Muslim or otherwise, are perfectly aware of that themselves. That remains important, naturally. But what are they supposed to do then, when they have no money of their own? It's easy for women with an income to be critical, they don't have to accept the pressure. But the rest are all slaves, nothing more.'

I sat down for tea with Elif Shafak, who combines her life as a writer in Istanbul with an academic career in the United States. She was very heavily pregnant at the time and was on the phone almost constantly; she had herself suddenly become fair game in the hounding of writers and journalists who supposedly insulted the 'Turkish identity'. This time, however, the nationalists were going out on a limb: it wasn't Shafak herself standing trial, in fact, but a character in one of her novels, a fictional

127

Armenian woman who had said, 'I am the grand-child of a family whose children were slaughtered by the Turkish butchers.'

That was the talk of the day, but afterwards we turned nonetheless to the striking results of that Gallup poll. Of course, Islam does contain certain anti-female elements, Shafak said, and those did not disappear when Turkey modernised and became a secular state. 'In Turkey, modernisation was first and foremost an experiment, designed by the elite, in effecting social change through government policies.' And that elite – which consisted largely of men – thereby left a vivid mark on public life and on what they themselves called 'the national story'. Within that context she warned me about the bridge: 'Don't forget, the bridge is and always has been a male culture and its story will always be a male story, even when it's about the repression of women. When men aren't busy repressing, they're out to save, to be the hero.'

That brought us straight to Pierre Loti, the pathological nineteenth-century seducer/rescuer of women. 'Yes, in fact one can sometimes speak of a "Loti complex",' Shafak believed. She saw it as a manifestation of old Western feelings of superiority. 'Muslim women always seem to elicit feelings of pity in Western men, no matter what their political bent: whether they're Orthodox Christians or left-wing liberals or feminists. They view all Muslim women as walking headscarves, as a single homo-geneous and repressed group that can only free itself by embracing Western values. They're always out to save those women – as though the women aren't capable of doing that themselves, and haven't in fact been doing exactly that for some time now.'

The head nurse had one more sister, the youngest of the three, but with her there was no need for secret encounters. She was, as it turned out, a devout, heavily veiled Muslim, but one who insisted time and again that she led a modern life, with a good husband and three fantastic children. Religion was an enrichment, she said, not a restriction. 'Things are going well for us, Allah be praised. We grant our daughters the freedom they need, they don't wear a headscarf the way I do and they'll be allowed to marry whomever they like. But they also have to respect the limits, especially when it comes to sex, drugs and the Internet.'

She was not on good terms with her oldest sister, whom she found self-obsessed, with her endless talk of a divorce that she never went through with. 'Tension is normal within a marriage. All over the world, men hold the hegemony. My husband and I have always tried to find common ground. Well, actually, I'm the one who's always tried to do that. I had to explain a lot to him. And sometimes there are things you simply don't do, for the children's sake. Your entire married life revolves around love, reason and respect. That's right, my headscarf too. It's an expression of love.'

When we asked her about the way she dressed she thought that was silly. That had nothing to do with her character. 'Before I got married I was just like my sisters. I wore miniskirts, did anything I felt like. I'm still that same woman. I chose for . . . well, you share your life with someone, it was a sign of respect. I've never seen it as a restraint or a form of repression. On the contrary, it's my free choice, my democratic right.' She began talking about her daughters again, two emancipated girls, according to her. That had been her doing, she said: 'I shaped them; they're free now.'

Later the two older sisters told me the story of a beautiful young girl, clever, independent, the only one who could handle their father. She had long blonde hair, long legs, she wore tight jeans, she was so free, freer than anybody else. That had been their little sister, once. Her mother died when she was ten and she got married at nineteen. Her husband was quite a bit older, but he promised her everything she wanted. He had money, a nice house on the coast, what more could she want? She married him and was trapped. She had to pray five times a day, she wasn't allowed to leave the house, and she had a live-in mother-in-law who terrorised the household. 'The old witch even forbade her to have sex: "He's my son, you're making him too tired!" ' Her father tried to help her, the couple moved away, the father died. 'After that there was no one left on the outside to support her, she had no job, no economic independence. We couldn't help her either, we were too busy dealing with our own problems.'

The older sister: 'He became abusive, she went from one depression to another, and meanwhile they made three children. She blamed us for talking her into that marriage and I'm afraid she was right. She was actually in love with someone else, a boy who didn't have a job at the time, who still had to do his military service. But when that respectable older gentleman appeared we thought he was the ideal match. My father felt exactly the same way. What a disaster.

'If our little sister had had a job she'd probably be divorced now. And without that headscarf, of course, it would have been much easier for her to find one. That's the way all these old preconceptions keep each other going.'

The head nurse: 'These days she claims she's happy, but that's only for the sake of her children. So she tries to be happy herself, there's nothing else she can do but try with all her might. All that anger inside her, that breaks everyone's heart.'

To complete matters, the old bridge caught fire on

16 May 1992, then seemed to disappear for all time. In actual fact, however, it still existed. Late one afternoon the pavement photographer told us that the whole thing had simply been towed upriver and still stood rusting away a few kilometres to the north-west. We decided to go immediately. It was a long walk, first past the fish market, then across the fields where, people say, a great many guilty acts take place by night and where, by day, all and sundry lay sleeping off whatever needed sleeping off, then on past the little tin mills, the dealers in metal shears and drills, the storage yards for rust and iron pipes, the fishing housefathers, drunkards and young people at the riverside, and in the water dozens of boats, iron, wood, rotted and brand-new, lone planks, a dog's cadaver covered in algae, hundreds of empty bottles. The old bridge had experienced a brief resurrection as light-blue link between two suburbs, but now it lay abandoned once more, replaced by yet another modern span a little further along. These days the bridge was permanently open, its central pontoons bobbing lonely beside the two enormous abutments.

Seeing it like this made me feel strange, rather like looking at a corpse lying in state. Vereinigte Maschiner Fabriken, Augsburg–Nürnberg. I recognised every detail: the stairs, the iron pattern along the railings, the graceful arc lamps, everything I had seen time and time again in all those photographs was suddenly there before me. Climbing the stairs, the used hypodermic needles crunched beneath your feet; there, at least, a form of nightlife still went on. For the rest, however, everything was barricaded and welded shut: the restaurants where the city's chroniclers had sat and watched, the coffeehouse of Master Ali, Uncle Hüseyin and Grandpa Mehmet, the landing stages where the poor folk had cheered the arrival of the bluefish, the factory girls' pavements, the lamp-post marking the spot where the last sultan was given his ticket.

Darkness fell as we were walking back. On the bridge, everyone had packed up. Only the bookseller remained. I never once saw an eager student leaf through one of his volumes. He simply sat there in that abandoned, draughty corridor, on his shop floor consisting of eight old newspapers.

The Storm of the Fish

The conquest, or fall, of Byzantium took place on 29 May 1453. Eleven days later, on 9 June, three small ships packed with refugees sailed into the Venetian harbour of Chania on the island of Crete – a sailor shouted to the watch there that the 'king of cities' had fallen to 'the Turkish Antichrist'. It took that long for the news to reach a Western outpost. On 29 June, precisely one month after the fact, the first messengers arrived in Venice itself with the news. And it was not until late July that the evil tidings reached the courts of Scandinavia and Scotland: two whole months.

The attack on the World Trade towers in New York took place on 11 September 2001. Most of the world watched and experienced the event with their own eyes. It concerned everyone on earth, it drove us together and apart, and the sparks flew in all directions.

Out of the blue, a new boy had appeared over by one of the abutments. He was from the countryside, freshly discharged from the army, and this was his first day on the bridge. He was standing beside a set of bathroom scales, as he had been since seven in the morning. It was now eleven o'clock and we were his first customers. Half a million. He was twenty-two, the oldest of nine brothers and sisters;

his father had died six months earlier and now the family was trying its luck in Istanbul. But there were no jobs here either: the entire textile industry was in the process of moving to China. One of his sisters had found work and the family lived on three hundred and fifty million a month. Hunger? He shrugged. 'Allah will help us. It's all we have.'

Not so very long ago he and his siblings would all have found jobs quickly enough in the large factories at the edge of town, the kind of simple manufacturing work that Western Europe had largely shrugged off at the end of the last century: textiles, metal, assembly lines et cetera. These days the people on the bridge are in direct competition with Chinese farmers; a battle which, by the look of it, they are bound to lose. The Turkish economy is booming, a city the likes of Barcelona or Tel Aviv is rising across the Bosporus, but it seems they will once again fall between two stools. For no matter how poor the rest of the country may be, the cost of living in a new metropolis like this can only rocket.

'No one in the village could help us. There was nothing for us there.' He had a bright face and calm eyes. As always, the bridge thundered and shook. Two hours later he was gone. We never saw him again.

The season arrived for the Storm of the Fish, which

blows in around the end of October and was once known for bringing huge schools of tuna into the Bosporus. But that was long ago. The storks had returned south from Europe. The old Spanish couple stood shivering, smoking a cigarette. Their dog lay in its basket beneath a piece of sailcloth. They had no raincoats; her woollen jumper was heavy with rain, but she didn't mind. With a boat of their own they had tried to set off for a better fishing spot, but couldn't get the motor started. Now she's hatched a plan to become a tourist guide: 'How do you say that in English: "an hour and then one half"?' By the loos, where the insole vendor was sitting, the air was moist and warm. The television drowned out all conversation. His friend the bookseller had recently moved to a smaller pied-à-terre: he wasn't sure how he was going to pay the rent, or pay for his daughter's education.

Önder had disappeared without a trace. He had either been arrested or had headed for the beaches at Izmir, no one knew which. Perhaps, at some airport twenty years from now, I will run into him again in the guise of a wealthy entrepreneur. Good business, shady business, he has it all in him.

The old porter recited the lyrics of a song: 'I cannot get what I want / but I do not complain.' Dejectedly, he mumbled something about being only 'half a man'. 'The Turkish economy has gone to the dogs,' he said as he rearranged his wares –

two pairs of trousers and a shoe-and-a-half. 'There will be another military dictatorship soon, mark my words.'

Meanwhile, we had survived a minor bombing. The bridge is a city in miniature and it had been only a matter of time before something like that happened here. When the dull concussion came that bright, sunny morning, everyone knew immediately what it meant. Down on the steps and along the ferry landing people were screaming, within seconds there was no one left on the quay – except for a few of the wounded.

There had been a bombing here once before, in a restaurant next door to the Galata Café. This time they had blown up a rubbish bin at the foot of the steps to the bus station, where families always sat waiting later in the day. The damage was relatively slight. Three people had been taken to hospital, and by lunchtime the bomb experts and television crews were already packing their things. I stood watching from behind the police cordon, along with a local cameraman. 'We're in deep shit again,' he grumbled. 'Inside all those cans of worms you Europeans are so keen on opening there are many hidden tensions; in that respect this is just like Iraq. And it could turn into just as bad a mess. But you people in the West wouldn't know about that.'

Then came the evenings of Ramadan and the atmosphere on the bridge was just like Christmas, the same festive feeling, the same cosiness, the same craving for warmth and food. Cheerful as always, the voice of the lottery-ticket girl echoed through the gallery of shops. A rowdy group of drug users stormed her table, trying to lay their hands on one final ticket. She talked them down valiantly. 'It's their last hope. I know them.' It hadn't been a bad day: she hadn't sold many big tickets, but the little scratch cards were going fast. 'They've given me new pills,' she whispered. 'They really help the anger inside me.'

Most of the people on the bridge, even the 'humanists', stuck strictly to the rules of Ramadan. They ate only after sunset, but . . . as soon as the signal is given the bridge is transformed into a huge, hungry mouth. Whole meals suddenly appeared from nowhere, waiters and errand boys began running back and forth, in every nook and cranny there were pedlars, shoeshine boys and pickpockets raking it in; in every shop you saw bosses and staff sitting down to eat together; the bridge, if only briefly, shut its mouth and chewed. The feast seemed to take place in the same monochrome that characterised the old photographs of the bridge, dozens of which I had seen, their details etched in my memory. At times the inhabitants of today's bridge seem as dislocated as the old bridge lying upstream. Lisbon revels in its *saudade*, but here they have their *hüzün*, a gentle brand of melancholy in which the city dwellers bask, a mood that has, with the years, become fused with the city itself, however modern it may sometimes seem.

You can tell from the muted tones: with the exception of the occasional flame motif, today's bridge goes dressed in blacks, browns and greys. There is almost nothing left of the bright green, orange, red, gold, yellow, blue and turquoise that Edmondo de Amicis saw crossing the bridge in 1878. Orhan Pamuk has written of a 'black and white' feeling with which present-day Istanbullus experience their city, a lack of colour that perfectly matches their intense wistfulness and the diffidence that goes with it.

Wistfulness is a sweetish kind of mourning, and mourning is an expression of loss, not least of all a loss of certainties. Those certainties, once, were founded on the amazing continuity of the imperial Roman city of Constantinople where, for more than a thousand years, a dynasty of ninety-two emperors ruled over the greatest and most important metropolis in Europe. It was, in retrospect, upon just such continuity that the ostensible Ottoman calm was built, that sated richness of palaces and summer villas in which everything seemed fixed and unchangeable for all time.

Yet for the West this same city, which sailors on 9 June 1453 without a second thought still spoke of as 'the king of cities', had become a remote corner of the world: a prosperous and dynamic remote corner, but a remote corner nonetheless. And that is what it gradually came to be, more and more, in the eyes of its inhabitants themselves – even when the time needed to travel to Vienna and Marseilles first shrank from weeks to days, and then to hours. During the second half of the twentieth century, while Europe was experiencing a miracle of mass prosperity, grand Istanbul sank further and further into isolation and obscurity. Growing uncertainty undermined the citizens' self-confidence, concepts such as 'honour', 'pride' and 'the nation' became entrenched in them with an ever-increasing inflexibility, and at the same time there was that constant sense of ambiguity and contingency.

In the space of a century and a half the bridge changed appearances no less than five times. The face of old Istanbul deteriorated, one after the other the wooden houses rotted and caught fire, and large sections of the old city rapidly became overgrown with a tangle of tower blocks. Not a single one of the wooden homes that filled the enormous Ottoman capital in the sixteenth and seventeenth centuries is still standing. In 1854, Théophile Gautier sailed over the Bosporus past an endless parade of summer palaces, painted apple-green and shaded by plane trees, each one lovelier than the last. More than a century later a youthful Orhan Pamuk saw one wooden villa after another burst into flame; he and his friends piled into cars and drove down to the shores of the Bosporus in order not to miss the spectacle; they played Creedence Clearwater Revival on the car stereo, drank tea and beer, ate toasted cheese sandwiches and watched as the final remnants of the Ottoman Empire went to ruin.

The city's cosmopolitan character eroded further and further. In September 1955, when tensions surrounding the island of Cyprus reached such a pitch that war almost broke out between Turkey and Greece, the 'rabble' was released for the last time. All non-Turkish shops along the streets of Pera were plundered by a baying mob, refrigerators – a sign of great prosperity at that time – were dragged down the hillside, the large round cheeses of the Greek grocers rolled down the streets and when it was all over the pavement glistened with broken glass. More Greeks left the city after that than in 1453. Of the quarter of a million Greeks who had lived here in 1914, in 2006 barely two thousand remained. According to its elderly and unsalaried editor-in-chief, *Apoyevmatini*, Istanbul's only remaining Greek-language daily newspaper, has exactly five hundred and twenty readers.

'Nothing remains what it is, not even our hearts,' the poet Ahmet Muhip Diranas once wrote. 'But how can a city grown fat with centuries / Faster even than a human life / Disappear so quickly?'

Istanbul had always been a city of comings and

goings, a straightforward-thinking city with, as Joseph Brodsky noted, a certain carelessness towards the past, a city of disposable houses and disposable neighbourhoods. In the twentieth century that urge for permanent change and adaptation became a value in itself. Within a little less than a hundred years the traditional, multi-ethnic, multi-religious Ottoman Empire had been transformed into a modern, secular nation state, and the city was transformed along with it. The driving force behind that revolution was an elite who desired affiliation with Western culture, whatever the cost, and would have liked to see all memories of the East obliterated.

The success of those efforts to knead Turkey into a new social mould is open to debate, but the ambition and adaptability of both city and country were and are astounding. To the countries bordering the Black Sea, Istanbul has once again become 'The City', the opportunities are enormous; if Turkey ever joins the European Union, it might easily become a new Byzantium, '*the* metropolis' of south-eastern Europe and the Near East. And because of its radical modernity it will be a city largely cut off from its own historical roots.

Elif Shafak spoke in this context of 'collective amnesia', an attitude to life that facilitated social change but at the same time obstructed all historical awareness – to say nothing of the ability to look back critically over the past. Pamuk wrote of his 'slippery, contradictory thoughts' about the city, of 'not quite belonging to this place, and not quite [being] a stranger'.

The poverty, too, is of a different kind from that in other major cities. Each and every day, after all, a thousand and one details – palaces, but also the final rotting remains of once-beautiful villas – confront the city's inhabitants with the painful loss of a unique culture and an empire that was, by all accounts, impressive. All reference to the cultural *richesse* and diversity of the Ottomans is usually looked upon askance: it is a 'right-wing' thing to do, the left feels; it is 'not modern', feels the right; it is 'not done', feels almost everyone. Case closed. Historical objects – with the exception of a few official monuments – are not cherished here. They are painful truths, pangs of nostalgia, between which one attempts to smooth out the wrinkles of modern existence as well as one can.

It was a late Sunday afternoon, darkness was drawing in. The Black Wind had picked up again, the thermometer made it only a few notches past zero. The newspapers told of heavy snow clouds on their way from Germany and the Balkans. The cold wind blew along the gutters of the old Greek neighbourhood, up and down the hillsides, around the ruins of the elegant mansions, past the sagging bay windows, the flapping curtains, the lone bakery, the crying babies, the dimly lit cake and soap shops on the street corners. Little girls were out skipping, or doing something complicated with a long piece of elastic. The boys played football, or clattered along after me on their roller skates across the paving stones: 'Hello! Hello!'

I had said my goodbyes. The lottery girl had given me a free ticket, the insole vendor and the bookseller had given me a hug. No one was out on the bridge any more, even the insole vendor had stayed at home, the only fishing pole in use was that of the man from the bank, but for him being cold was part of the sport. The rest of them were watching television, they were sitting in the coffeehouse, they were lying in bed and dreaming their dreams: the head nurse of a visa to see her grandchild; the bookseller of a good marriage for his daughter; the waiter of his son becoming a professional footballer; the perfume seller of the grass around the village of his youth; the blind flautist of murdering his ex-wife; the tea vendor of two thousand dollars to buy a truck and set up a transport-cum-smuggling business in his village; the umbrella salesman of taking the whole of England to court; the insole vendor of a cheerful meal with all his children; the oldest sister of a divorce; the policeman whose beat the bridge was of a TV course, a diploma, a better pay grade and then retirement; the lottery girl of her sister performing as a backing singer on a television programme – and the man with the drum was still far away.

It grew colder. The coloured laundry flapped on lines across the narrow streets. Smoke crawled low through the neighbourhood, people everywhere were busy scavenging for wood, the men sawed and chopped, splinters flew, in the darkness of the basement homes the fires in the plate-metal stoves were glowing red.

At dusk the rain slowly turned to wet snow and then the flakes began to fall, white and regal; above the Blue Mosque even the flying souls were gone from sight.

Acknowledgements

I would never have been able to do my work in Istanbul without the sensible counsel of Bernard Bouwman and Elif Shafak, the comradeship and unflagging efforts of my daily interpreter Mehmet Onur Zor, and the candour and trust of Ali Özbagriaçik (the insole vendor), Mehmet Ince (the bookseller), Önder Karabuga (the cigarette boy), Ömer Ihtiyar (the old porter), Ayhan and Fatma (the elderly Spanish couple), and all the other people who talked to me on the bridge.

In Holland, Hanneke van der Heijden and Margreet Dorleijn were willing to translate for me even the most curious of texts by a host of city chroniclers. All the translated sections upon which the original version of this book was based, including previously existing translations, were done by them.

My publisher, Emile Brugman, was a source of constant encouragement. René van Stripriaan provided numerous suggestions in the course of editing the manuscript. I would like to thank all of them from the bottom of my heart.

The list of names of various winds and storms I received from John Freely, who garnered them at the fishermen's café Nazmi in Bebek.

The image of the bridge as a bird's body comes from the urban chronicler Nâzim Hikmet.

The English version of the poem 'The Bridge' ('*Köpru*') by Said Faik is an adaptation based on the Dutch translation by Hanneke van der Heijden.

Elif Shafak has since been acquitted. The occasional name and description has been changed to protect the privacy of those who talked to me.

Bibliography

Akcam, Taner, *De Armeense genocide* (Amsterdam, 2007)

Baade, Klaus, *Europa in Bewegung, Migration vom späten 18. Jahrhundert bis zur Gegenwart* (Münich, 2000)

Bowman, James, *Honor, A History* (New York, 2006)

Boyeunca, Caglar, *Istanbul Görünümleren* (Istanbul, 1971)

Braudel, Fernand, *A History of Civilisations* (Paris, 1987/London, 1993)

Brodsky, Joseph, 'Flight from Byzantium' in *Less Than One: Selected Essays* (New York, 1986)

Celik, Zeynep, *The Remaking of Istanbul, Portrait of an Ottoman City in the Nineteenth Century* (Berkeley, USA, 1986)

Cöker, Fahri, *De bruggen van de Gouden Hoorn* (Istanbul, 1986)

Dalrymple, William, *From the Holy Mountain, A Journey in the Shadow of Byzantium* (London, 1997)

De Amicis, Edmondo, *Constantinople* (New York, 1896)

Freely, John, Istanbul (London, 2003)

Gallup World Poll, 'What Women Want: Listening to the Voices of Muslim Women' in *International Herald Tribune* (9 June 2006)

Gautier, Théophile, *Constantinople* (Paris, 1873)

Heijden, Hanneke van der and Margreet Dorleijn (eds), *Moderne Turkse verhalen* (Amsterdam, 2005)

Hinrichs, Jan Paul et al., *Passage Istanbul* (Amsterdam, 2001)

Isin, Ekrem, *Everyday Life in Istanbul: Social Historical Essays on People, Culture and Spatial Relations* (Istanbul, 2001)

Kuban, Dogan, *Istanbul, An Urban History* (Istanbul, 1996)

Leggewie, Claus (ed.), *Die Türkei und Europa* (Frankfurt am Main, 2004)

Lewin, Lisette, 'Gevaarlijke liefde tussen de tomben, Het dubbelleven van Pierre Loti in Stamboel' in Hinrichs et al., p. 48

Lithgouw, Willem, *Lant-Reyse, Uyt Schotlant nae de vermaerde deelen des Werelts* (Amsterdam, 1653)

Loti, Pierre, *Aziyadé en Fantôme d'Orient* (Paris, 1991)

—— *Constantinople in 1890* (Istanbul, 2002)

Mansel, Phillip, *Constantinople, City of the World's Desire, 1453–1924* (London, 1997)

Orga, Irfan, *Portrait of a Turkish Family* (New York, 1950)

Pamuk, Orhan, *The Black Book* (London, 1994)

—— *Istanbul, Memories and the City* (London, 2005)

—— 'The Anger of the Damned' in *The New York Review of Books* (48, no. 8, 15 November 2001)

Rosenthal, Steven T., *The Politics of Dependency, Urban Reform in Istanbul* (Westport, USA, 1980)

Shafak, Elif, *The Flea Palace* (London, 2005)

—— 'The de-feminisation of Turkish culture' in *Turkish Daily News* (30 July 2006)

—— *The Bastard of Istanbul* (New York, 2007)

Valkenstein, Kees, *In en om Stamboel* (Utrecht, 1909)

Wheatcroft, Andrew, *The Ottomans, Dissolving Images* (London, 1993)

Wortley Montagu, Lady Mary, *The Turkish Embassy Letters* (London, 1994)

Pont de Galata